FLYING SAIL

The Humber Keel *Comrade* preserved by the Humber Keel and Sloop Preservation Society under sail on the River Humber.
Mike Lawtry Photography.

The Humber sloop *Amy Howson* preserved by the Humber Keel and Sloop Preservation Society, pictured from the Humber Bridge.
Mike Lawtry Photography.

FLYING SAIL

HUMBER KEELS AND SLOOPS

by
Michael E. Ulyatt

dedicated to the memory of Capt. Fred Schofield

My. Pye
Books
1995

First published 1974 as a limited edition
by Bradley Publications, Hull.

This revised edition   ©   1995 Michael Ulyatt

published by
Mr. Pye (books)
47 Hailgate
Howden
Goole
DN14 7ST

ISBN 0 946289 30 1

CONTENTS

ACKNOWLEDGEMENTS

Whilst this book has been compiled almost exclusively from primary sources it is not intended as a comprehensive history of keels and sloops. It contains reminiscences by the last men to sail these boats as well as a collection of abstracts from contemporary records and newspapers.

Without the assistance of the following it would not have been written:-

The editors of the following media who published my letter appealing for information:

Hull Daily Mail, Yorkshire Post, Yorkshire Evening Press, Lincolnshire Echo, Bridlington Free Press, The Dalesman, Beverley Guardian, The Driffield Times, Lincolnshire Life, Sea Breezes, East Coast Digest, Yorkshire Gazette and Herald, Mariner's Mirror, Pocklington Times, Scunthorpe Star, Double Nine (Quarterly Magazine of the Pocklington Canal Amenity Society) and *Yorkshire Life*;

R. F. Smith of Barton-on-Humber, who organised meetings with some old keel and sloop skippers and supplied me with invaluable photographs;

Isabella B. Thompson, Curator of Goole Museum and Art Gallery which contains the Garside Collection, an excellent shipping display;

J. S. English, A.L.A., librarian at Gainsborough Public Library, who very kindly made available to me the library's collection of E. W. Carter's photographs and who supplied me with the extensive list of references used as a basis for the bibliography;

The Humber Keel and Sloop Preservation Society;

Norman Burnitt, photographer of Goole, who copied some of the Reuben Chappell paintings onto film;

The City of Sheffield Museums Department; Hull Museums; The National Maritime Museum; The Waterways Museum, Stoke Bruerne; John H. Whitaker of Hull; Lincoln and Hull Marine Contractors, Hull; The Castle Museum, York; Catherine M. Wilson, A.M.A., Curator of Lincolnshire Life in Lincoln;

G. Waites of Driffield and Horace Hunsley of Burton Fleming, who between them told me a great deal about the Driffield Canal and its history;

Staniland and Co., of Thorne; Clapson and Sons of Barton-on-Humber; Geoffrey W. Oxley, City Archivist, Hull; J. W. Griffin, Assistant Curator of Scunthorpe Museum;

The Inland Waterways Association, who put me in contact with canal photographer, Hugh McKnight of Shepperton;

J. B. Bradshaw, Director of Ferens Art Gallery, Hull;

Ron Lang, Secretary of Hull River Craft and Lighter Owners Association;

Hull Local History Library;

Captain Fred Schofield of Beverley, who had the rare good sense to keep old freight books, records and photographs relating to life on a sailing barge;

The photographic department of the *Hull Daily Mail*; Richard Lamb and John Valentine, who copied most of the old photographs used; Tom Hoy of Brough who kindly read my original draft; Lynn Sergeant who typed my manuscript; everyone who wrote to me and so readily gave information and lent me photographs;

Finally, to George Dickinson, Beverley-based reporter for the *Hull Daily Mail*, who, still unbeknown to him, first kindled my interest in the Humber Keel and Sloop by suggesting a book such as this at the end of his review of Harvey Benhem's book *Down Tops'l* reprint edition in the *Hull Daily Mail*, sometime in 1971.

March 1974

I am grateful to Mike Kemp of Mr. Pye Books for suggesting an update of my book. In the twenty years since publication, I have met some great characters and ended up editing *The Slabline*, the twice yearly magazine of the Humber Keel and Sloop Preservation Society and acting as its Publicity Officer. To Colin Screeton, Jim Thompson, John Hainsworth, Arthur Credland, Bill and Mary Wilson, the late Charlie Gray and George Fussey, Cedric Lodge, Dave Robinson, Cyril Harrison and all other 'preservationists', I say thank you.

For this reprint I have deliberately excluded the details of construction and rigging in the original edition in deference to the late Capt. Fred Schofield, whose descriptions in his book *Humber Keels and Keelmen* (Terence Dalton, 1988) can never be equalled.

Michael E. Ulyatt
August 1994

CHAPTER ONE — THE HUMBER KEEL

Keels leaving St. Andrew's Dock for Alexandra Dock on the River Humber
H. L. Cartlidge

The Humber Keel, with various modifications to its construction throughout the centuries, is thought to be a direct descendant of the Viking longboat.

In the year 449 A.D. the warrior brothers Hengist and Horsa sailed across the North Sea from Scandinavia with their armies in three 'ceolas' and landed on the east coast of England to plunder and pillage along the coastline of Kent. The marauding Vikings, in later years, penetrated inland to York along the Humber in very similar vessels.

Keels were recorded as a distinct class in the fourteenth century; in Tudor times York Corporation documents recorded that '*Ther is belonging to the said citie* [York] *ten vessels called Keylls – the which ar of thirty or forty tonnes.*'

A register of keels and sloops, dated 1795, and in the possession of Hull Corporation, lists vessels, names, masters, capacity and the number of men employed as crew. Several masters had boy apprentices bound to them for periods of 3, 4,

5 or 7 years. On the Hull to Leeds journey (100 miles or thereabouts) William Cooper had one weekly boy servant as mate, while John Rowbottom, on the Hull to Thorne route (50 miles), had one river- or boat-man as mate.

Also in the Hull Archives are Weighhouse account volumes registering cargo dues collected on lead shipped through the port of Hull in 1696. Robert Gleadhall, John Luddington and William Drayton used their keels solely for shipping lead which was weighed in pigs and stored in barrels. The Earl of Rutland shipped a great deal of ore through Hull via the canal system at the end of the seventeenth century.

An entry in the Hull General Quarter Sessions Records tells of a charge dated 21st November 1802 that:

> "*Robert Pinder, master of the sloop* **Friendship** *of Gainsborough and his mate James McDonald took the oath of theft, having been accused of not satisfactorily accounting for 50 bushels of salt from a*

Keels drying their sails after re-tanning. Lincoln Brayford, 1910.
W. E. R. Hallgarth

The Ellerman Wilson Line's *City of Paris* and a Humber keel, c.1945.
H. L. Cartlidge

Amy Howson leaving Yarborough Oil Mills at Brigg
under power on 27th July 1949.   *D. Shelton*

consignment of salt to Messrs. Blakeston and Co., Merchants of Hull.'

The charge, however, was not proven against the two men.

In 1822 there was a great storm in the south of England which lasted for seven days and which caused the River Rother in Sussex to change its course. Excavations carried out on the former river bed revealed a boat remarkably preserved in the mud and sand. It was identical in length, beam, depth, apparent rig and construction to the Humber keel and it was calculated to date from circa 1287.

With the opening of inland waterways in England in the late 1790's and the early to mid nineteenth century, the Humber keel really came into its own and became known as 'the workhorse of the river and canal.'

The nineteenth century keels were chiefly built of oak with pitch pine decks and memel bottom. Although a number were clench built, most were carval built with very bluff bows and stern and were designed in order to carry the maximum cargo and to give room for living space for the captain and crew.

The Humber keel could justly lay claim to the title of 'Yorkshire's own windjammer'. She had to be built strong enough to sail in the heavy cross currents of the Humber Estuary and on occasions along the east coast, but she also had to have a shallow enough draught to sail along rivers or canals whose depth of water was not very high. They were initially built of wood but later ones were made of iron and the last ones were constructed of steel. The size of a keel was determined by the size of locks which would be encountered; e.g. Barnsley, Sheffield, Manvers and Driffield size. The old wooden keels were built by eye, by craftsmen who scorned detailed plans and drawings. They were certainly built to last. The *North Cape* was built at Brigg in Lincolnshire in 1840 and was still carrying regular cargoes in 1912.

In 1900, Joseph Cooper of Hull ordered a new keel to be built by a Mr. Warren, who had keel building yards at Beverley and New Holland. It was Sheffield size, $61\frac{1}{2}$ft long, $15\frac{1}{2}$ft beam with a depth of 7ft 8in and a 1ft 9in sheer. Built of composite, the barge could carry 100 tons of cargo. Her cost was £500 less £200 in part exchange for Mr. Cooper's old keel *Friendship*.

Probably the busiest keel-building yard was Richard Dunston's at Thorne. Founded in 1858, a total of ninety-six keels were built there during the company's keel-building history. The yard turned out two keels every year on average and among well-known keels which were built there were *Britannia, Cathleen, Mayday, Dux, Daybreak, Elinor* and *Warrior*.

The family firm of Clapson began building keels at Barton-on-Humber in 1880. There had been a boatyard at Barton for over a thousand years. The many creeks in Lincolnshire were full

A keel being launched at Clapson's Yard, Barton-on-Humber in 1920.
W. E. R. Hallgarth

A skeleton of a keel on the stocks at Clapson's Yard, Barton-on-Humber in 1920.
W. E. R. Hallgarth

W. H. Harrison's yard,
Beverley, c.1910.
Author's collection

The launch of the keel *United*
at Parkgate Yard, Rotherham
in 1906.
W. Parish

11

A keel adapted for use as a floating drilling platform to make test borings for the Humber Bridge in 1930. At that time it was expected that the bridge would take a line to the east of Hessle and Barton.
R. F. Smith

The steel keel *Lady Ellen*, pictured at Torksey. Completed for Captain T. Tomlinson, White House, Torksey, by J. P. Watson, Steel Lighter, Barge and Steam Boat Builder of Gainsborough in November 1910. *Lady Ellen* was 74ft x 15ft 4in x 7ft 3in built complete to specification and model and cost £685. Payment was by credits. £100 by cheque on 31st May; £195 by cheque on 2nd August; £195 by cheque on 10th September, leaving a balance of £195.
Lincoln and Hull Marine Contractors Ltd.

of boatyards. The brickyards at Goxhill, Barrow, Ferriby, Killingholme and Skitter; the railway wharf at Winteringham; and Barton's brickyards, whiting mills, rope works and maltings were all tailor-made for accepting the keel as a quick, cheap and convenient method of transporting freights. The firm also built Humber sloops, the last one to be built there was *Peggy* in 1935.

Scarr's of Hessle Haven employed one hundred people during the hey-day of keel building and they could turn out six keels a year. Before the first world war, their keels cost around £600 to buy, whilst after the war prices rose to £1000, their secondhand value being £400.

Stanilands of Thorne began building keels in 1845 and became a very well-known yard but their keel-building virtually ended in 1914 and it was superseded by the sloop.

The following is a list of the better known boatbuilders, many of which closed as the use of the sailing barge declined:
Geo. Brown and Sons, Wilmington, Hull; Brown and Clapson, Barton-on-Humber; Burton's, Selby; R. Cliffe and Co., Castleford; Cottingham Bros., Goole; Day's, New Holland; Garlocks, Knottingley; Stephen Guest, Mexborough; Harrisons, Beverley; Hurst and Escreet, York; Kendalls, Lincoln; Dick Ledger, Wakefield; Lesters, Bassett Lock; Martin and Co., Humber Iron Works, Hull; Mellors, Brighouse; Thomas Pendlebury, Rotherham; Rainforth, Lincoln; Routh and Waddington, Winteringham; Ryders, Leeds; H. Scarr, Hessle; Joseph Scarr, Beverley; Scholey, Swinton; Smith and Sons, Louth; M. Thompson, Boston; Oliver Thompson, Knottingley; Thornton and Jackson, Mirfield; Turner, Hull; Waddington, Mexborough; M. Warmsworth, Sprodboro'; Warren's, New Holland; J. P. Watson and Co., Gainsborough; Wrays, Burton Stather; Worfolk, Knottingley.

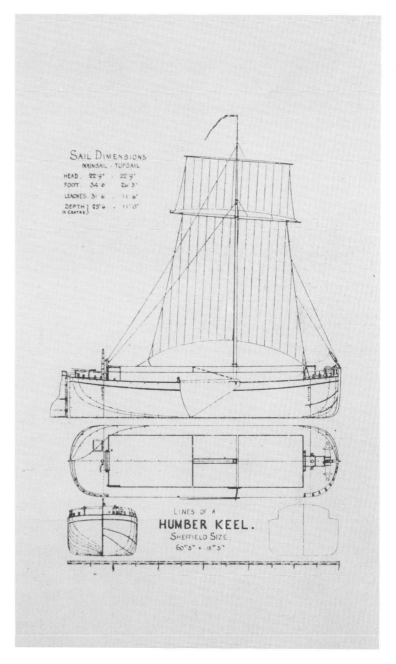

Plan of a Humber Keel

The *Kiero* winning the first race organised by the Hull Keel Regatta Club in 1874; oil painting by W. R. Nixon.
Hull Museums

CHAPTER TWO — THE HUMBER KEEL REGATTA

The Humber Keel Regatta was first held in 1874 and continued annually until 1903. The headquarters of the organising committee was the Minerva Hotel in Nelson Street, Hull. Brethren of Hull Trinity House and various local tradespeople would donate prizes and the interest aroused was tremendous. Crowds would line the quays and wharves along Hull's river front to see keelmen handle their boats superbly, competing with strong flowing tides and hazardous sandbanks; conditions which made the regatta on the River Humber an exciting contest.

The keels lined up at anchor off Humber Dock and a gun was fired from the second floor window of the Minerva Hotel signalling the start of the race. The craft set off down the Humber passing the mark boat off Victoria Pier, passing round the middle float, on the starboard hand and then returned to Hull passing the mark boat off Victoria Pier once again, also on the starboard hand. The race lasted three to four hours, depending on wind and tide. Each keel carried a crew of five for the race, two for'ard, two aft and one amidships. The winner of the first ever regatta was the *Kiero*.

During a visit to Hull's Maritime Museum, I came across a programme for the regatta of 1901, price 2d. Held on Tuesday 16th July, it had an entry of ten boats. The keels, their captains and owners were listed:

1	*Ivy*	J. Oliver	G. Fish
2	*Sympathy*	Geo. Matchatt	Geo. Matchatt
3	*William and Eliza*	Geo. Shaw	H. Sutton
4	*Change*	R. Dawson	R. Dawson
5	*Eleanor*	G. Fish	G. Fish
6	*Ethel*	J. Carter	J. Carter
7	*Ancholme*	M. Schofield	M. Schofield
8	*William Hewson*	Alf Hewson	Alf Hewson
9	*Argo*	W. Armstrong	W. Armstrong
10	*Friends*	J. Ward	J. Ward

The race committee:

Rob Mackie (Chairman); Herbert Sutton (Commodore); J. Moxon (Vice-Commodore); Chas. Burmeister (Umpire); W. Acaster, snr. (Vice-Chairman); Harry Smith (Treasurer); Col. Thorney, Geo. Barrass, F. Hope, S. Barrass, C. Brammer, J. Barraclough, Watson Sutton, R. Guest, J. H. Hall (Committee Members); Tom E. Featherstone (Secretary); W. Acaster, jnr. (Assistant Secretary).

HULL KEEL REGATTA 1875

The following account of the second day's event is taken from the *Hull News* of 7th August 1875.

Keel	Captain	Owner	Port
Minnie	T. Porter	Brigham and Co.	Beverley
Queen	R. Major	C. Thompson	Hull
Hope	J. Cox	E. Bolton	Hull
Emily	W. Sutton	W. Sutton	Thorne
Eva Hewson	F. Day	W. Hewson	Hull
Hannah and Harriet	W. Patrick	C. W. Briggs and Co.	Hull
Jane and Maria	C. White	G. Bailey	Hull
Mog	M. Schofield	J. Jaques	Mexboro'
Albert Edward	M. Brook	R. Collison	Hull
Lily Dale	J. Othick	W. Nettleton	Hull
Annie	E. Todd	E. Todd	Thorne
Wilsons	W. Alsop	W. Alsop	Thorne
Providence	T. Kay	T. Kay	Thorne
Victory	J. Major	J. Storr	Hull

The vessels were anchored in a line from the north shore in the above order. Many of them were so close together that several collisions occurred before they got underway. The most serious was that between the *Queen* and the *Hope*. The first-named vessel, in rounding, ran close up to the stern of the *Hope* and as the *Queen*'s anchor was hanging over the bow, the fluke went through the *Hope*'s boat and the two vessels were fastened together in a manner that for some time defied all efforts to separate them. Whilst they were in this position, the *Wilsons*, which had had a leeward position, got sail on and stood in to windward. She passed the *Hope*'s bow so close that the keel's anchor caught foul of her leeboard and thus for a full ten minutes the three vessels were held together by their anchors.

Eventually the *Queen* and then the *Wilsons* got clear and went on the course after the other keels, who were by this time halfway to Paull. One of the conditions of the race was that each keel should tow her boat and as the *Hope*'s boat had filled with water she was not in a position to start. However the committee, anxious that the vessel should compete, borrowed a boat and took it to the *Hope*. A start was then made but with the other keels fully five miles away, the case appeared hopeless for the

Hope. Owing to the committee's steamer being detained with the *Hope*, they were not sufficiently near enough to number six buoy to ascertain the order in which the keels rounded and so no accurate time was taken. The first vessel round was the *Hannah and Harriet* at about forty-eight minutes past twelve, the start having been effected at 11.30 am. At the time the bulk of the vessels were passing the buoy, the *Hope* was seen coming along, at least eight miles up the river but with a fair wind and tide she soon got down and having got down she rounded the buoy and kept well over to windward. As the keels came up the Humber they had to stem the ebb tide which set them all rapidly to leeward, except the *Hope*, which kept well over to the Yorkshire coast and got a good lead up in the slack tide. Eventually, however, she began to drift to leeward and by the time she arrived on the Lincolnshire side of the river she was nearly a mile ahead of all the rest and bets were freely made on her ultimate success.

In coming about to stand to windward, the ill-luck which attended her at starting, again befell her for she missed stays, gathered sternway and went onshore. Her crew let go her anchor to prevent her driving further on and she was thus disqualified. Shortly afterwards the *Hannah and Harriet*, which held the leading position, had the misfortune to carry away her mainyard and she had to be towed up to Hull. The *Wilsons* then became the leading keel and she maintained her position to the end of the race, the flag boat being passed as follows:-

Wilsons, time 15 hours, 18 minutes, 58 seconds — Keel Regatta Club prize £50;
Victory, 5hr 24m 15s — Hull Merchants prize £13;
Albert Edward, 5hr 25m 45s — Hull Corporation prize £9;
Queen, 5hr 26m 5s — The Keelmen's prize £6;
Providence, 5hr 26m 15s — The Roundwood prize £3;
Emily, 5hr 31m 30s;
Jane and Maria, 5hr 35m 50s; and
Eva Hewson, 5hr 40m 34s — all had their entrance fee returned as their prizes.

The *Annie* and *Mog* arrived in the next ten minutes and both the *Minnie* and the *Lily Dale* some time later. The *Victory* passed the committee boat with her mainsail half lowered and of course, had it been fully up, she would have passed a little earlier. The committee steamer then returned to the Corporation Pier, the company on board being fully satisfied with their day's outing. In addition to the pleasure afforded by watching the keels, luncheon was provided for the visitors and a band played music at intervals.

CHAPTER THREE — THE HUMBER SLOOP

The Humber Sloop was built identically to a Humber Keel but the rigging was entirely different. Their usual length was between 65 feet and 68 feet with a beam of between 14ft 10in and 17ft 3in. She was a gaff and boom type craft with a foresail; the mast was set further forward than that of a keel and it carried two large triangular sails of the fore and aft rig which could be raised and lowered. The tiny fo'c'sle was usually used as a store while the handspike windlass occupied the extreme bow.

The sloop was certainly easier to handle than a keel on tideway. They sometimes sailed out of the River Humber along the east coast to Bridlington, the Wash, Yarmouth or Lowestoft but were usually confined to riverwork and did not often venture far up a canal. The usual crew, as on a keel, was a captain and mate, man or boy, although sometimes the captain's wife acted as mate.

The sloop *Phyllis* off Read's Island
in the River Humber.
H. L. Cartlidge

The sloop *Yokefleet* on the River Humber.
Author's collection

The laden sloop *Ivie*
R. F. Smith.

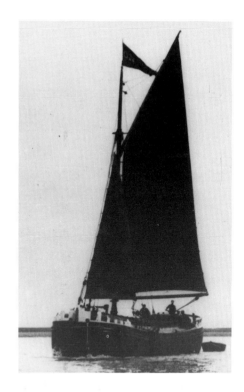

The sloop *Onward* on
the River Humber.
H. L. Cartlidge.

The sloop *Mystery* on the
River Humber.
H. L. Cartlidge.

The sloop *Lucy*.
Hull Museums.

The steel sloop *Kama* on the River Trent.
E. W. Carter Collection, Gainsborough Public Library.

The sloop *Rosalie Stamp* at the Horse Wash in Hull.
Hull Daily Mail.

Humber sloops *Rosalie Stamp* and *Burgate* at the Horse Wash in Hull.
R. F. Smith.

The sloops *Bee* and *Annie Maud* on the River Humber.
H. L. Cartlidge

The traditional 'raising of the flag' at the completion of the sloop *Mafeking*
at the Barton shipyard of Brown and Clapson in May 1900.
Her first skipper was T. Barraclough.   *R. Clapson*

The heavy timbers forming the skelton of the hull of the sloop *Peggy*,
the last sloop to be built at Clapson and Son's Yard at
Barton-on-Humber in 1935.   *W. E. R. Hallgarth*

Sloops *Burgate* and *New Clee* on the stocks at Clapson's Yard,
Barton-on-Humber in 1926.
W. E. R. Hallgarth

A number of sloops were used as 'sanders'. After sailing out they would wait for low tide when their flat bottoms enabled them to lie flush on the bed. The captain and his mate would jump overboard with large tins and scoop up the sand from the river bed. The water drained from holes pierced in the base and sides of the tins and the contents were then thrown into the hold until a full load was collected. The richer sloop owners had a gin wheel rigged up on the boom which was hove into the air. A wire on the winch came forward through the block to a leather bag fastened to a long pole. The mouth of the bag was lined with iron to keep it open. By dragging the bag and hoisting it aboard sand could be collected much quicker than by the 'tin method'.

The areas known for sand and gravel were Blacktoft or Cliff End for Trent sand (which was always called "haul-ups"); Paull, where the sand was very fine; Spurn 'Binks', gravel beds which extended out into the North Sea; Howden Dyke and Swinefleet Rack.

The sand and gravel was brought back to Hull and offered for sale, from the sloop, by the captain to local corporations, builders merchants or building contractors. In 1906, Captain G. W. Burkill, Master of the sloop *Providence*, sold 95 tons of sand at Goole, for £5/19/6p (£5.97½).

"There's Dandy Jack in Swinefleet Rack,
And Walt's on Cobbler's Hill,
My eye, my eye says Bugle Eye,
I've been a jolly fool,
I been right up the Howden Dyke
When I might have stopped at Goole."
An old sanders' song.

A sloop fully laden under a night sky on the River Humber.
H. L. Cartlidge.

The sloop *Bee* on the River Humber.
H. L. Cartlidge.

The sloop *Broomfleet* underway on the River Humber.
Author's collection.

The sloop *Sprite* off Barton Haven on the River Humber. *Sprite*, skippered by Jack Chant, was one of the last sloops under commercial sail. *R. F. Smith.*

The sloop *Ivie* against the evening sky after loading at Hoe Hill brickyard, Barton-on-Humber. *R. F. Smith.*

Regattas on the Humber were revived after 1918. There were few keels about then and the sloop race came into prominence. As many as twenty-five sloops took part. The start was off Barton Flats, continued round the middle light vessel off Grimsby if the tide was on the ebb during the morning; if not they raced round the Upper Whitton. As in the Keel Regattas the sloops carried a crew of five and there was an entrance fee of 10/-(50p). The sloops drew for position and lined up at anchor. One gunshot to be ready and two to be off, fired from the committee boat and the race was under way. Depending on wind and tide, the duration of the race was between three and five hours and the winner received a medallion and a side of bacon and he was permitted to carry a brass cockerel aloft for the following year to signal his achievement. The last man home received a booby prize.

The event was usually held on a Saturday and included wooden, iron and steel built sloops; the wooden ones receiving a thirty minute start because they were slower through the water. Tugs stood by in case any sloops became becalmed.

In 1926, Norman Barraclough, then a youth of 16, was one of the crew of the *Alva-S* which won the Regatta. Her skipper was Jack Simpson and they received a gold and silver medal for their victory. The *Alva-S* was later renamed the *Christine*, switching to engine power and operating out of Beverley Beck.

Beverley sloopman David Holgate took part in the 1927 Regatta when Jack Foster skippered the winning sloop, *Saxby*. David finished seventh with *Friendship*; later recounting to me how much he enjoyed the evening's celebrations in Barton, a tradition at the end of the race. Six sloops entered the Regatta in 1928 with Harry Hodgson coming in first with *Faxfleet*. David also recalled a character named Jack Richardson, known as 'Lucky Jack' because, although he never won a race, he always seemed to have favourable winds or channels.

The last Sloop Regatta took place in 1929.

David Holgate's sloop *Friendship* in the 1926 Humber Sloop Regatta.   *Author's collection*

The start of the last Humber Sloop Regatta on the River Humber in 1929.   *R. F. Smith*

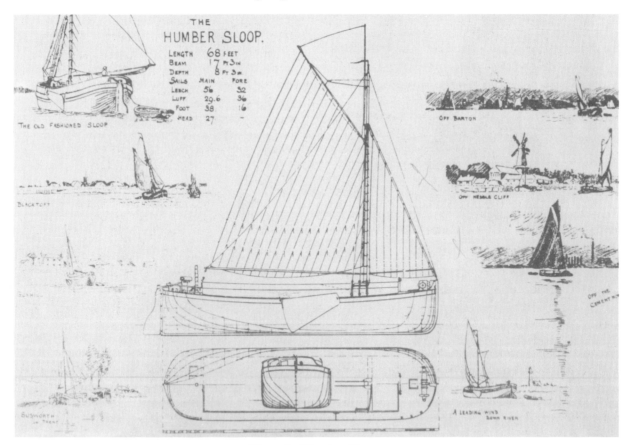

Plan of a Humber Sloop.

CHAPTER FIVE — KEEL AND SLOOP MEN

The keel *Annie Maud*, one reef in mainsail, at Thorne on the Stainforth and Keadby Canal, c.1930. Her captain, Fred Schofield, is seen on top of the hatches. The keel's owners were Robinson Bros of Town Mills, Rotherham. At the tiller is Jack Williamson, Captain Schofield's regular purchase-man. *Author's collection*

The keel and sloop skippers were excellent sailors, always alive to the many and varied conditions to be met under sail on rivers and canals. His mate was invaluable and they were a team, two against wind and tide. Their dress was usually dark corduroys, dark blue jersey (or guernsey) with two pearl buttons at the neck, white neckerchief and strong shoes or boots.

As well as knowing tide times, a skipper had to learn the different draughts of water encountered, facts which were passed down to each generation. With no compass to guide them, sailing was often difficult, especially on winter nights with fog and ice prevalent. One captain, asked by a foreign seaman if he carried radar, replied "Yes. I stand at the bow, in fog or at night, and throw stones in front. If there's a splash then we're afloat, if not, then we're aground."

Keel and sloop men were usually honest, straightforward and trustworthy. Some very extremely religious and superstitious characters. They believed bad luck would befall them if they sailed on a Sunday, went through rigging between two shrouds, lost their cap on deck, if the hold ladder was the wrong way up or if the stowers or boathooks were the wrong way round.

There was plenty of friendly rivalry among crews, both in searching for cargoes and in trying to win the race to their destination while under sail. This was really business competition but a close affinity existed among crews and they would help each other with loading and unloading or in any emergency.

The main cargoes carried were coal, wheat, firewood, gravel, oats, oil cake, bricks, tiles, cement, chalk, steel, barley and flour;

they also carried sugar beet, wire rods, beans, rye, cheese, soap, fruit, iron ore, limestone, cotton seed, wool and manure.

Payment was divided into "thirds". The owner took one third of the price the cargo fetched and he was responsible for maintenance of the keel or sloop. Out of his two thirds, the captain had to pay the mate's wages, food, loading and unloading charges, any towing or horse hiring fees, pilotage costs if incurred and dock dues. He would pay the owner his share on completion of the journey. Most craft operated this simple system but gravel cargo was usually shared 50/50.

Skippers and mates were alive to the temptations of poaching along the river or canal banks. They made baskets to catch eels, while to catch a salmon was a rare treat. Five keelmen once caught a salmon in the upper Humber and sold it in a pub for 6/-(30p) and the skipper divided the proceeds as "2/- (10p) for you, 2/- for you two and 2/- for me too".

With his wife and family often living on board or joining him for a trip, a skipper could keep his food bill low by living off the land. Wild fruits, swedes, turnips, carrots and cabbage varied the diet. Farmers in the late nineteenth century found movement of produce difficult to arrange. Since there was little passing trade it was not unusual for them to sell eggs at 1/- (5p) for 24 and the butter was plentiful. However life on board without a family could be very lonely and this tended to breed a quiet and philosophical approach to life.

Once a year, a skipper would lay up his vessel for two weeks for painting and general tidying up. Plenty of paint, linseed and

The Verity family of Driffield on board their keel *Speculat* on the Driffield Canal in 1910.
G. Waites

The keel *Edward* being poled up the River Hull below Stoneferry with 75 tons of coal from New Monkton, near Barnsley, Skipper Thomas Claxton. When tides were low keels had to be worked up the River Hull by stowers, c.1910.
Collection of Hugh McKnight Photography

Keel's cog boats, propelled by hand, two persons per boat. Stainforth Aquatic Sports just prior to World War One, Stainforth and Keadby Canal.
Author's Collection

Humber keel *Edward*. Start of a trip from Elland to Shepley Bridge and back, organised by the Salvation Army as a childrens' outing in 1911. West Yorkshire Capt. Claxton standing on the left. Power used was one horse.
Collection of Hugh McKnight Photography

tar was brought out, the sails would be re-tanned (the Grimsby Coal Salt and Tanning Company did this in Lincolnshire) and the decks, sides, hold and mast would be scrubbed thoroughly and re-varnished. Most keel and sloop owners and their families had an enormous pride in keeping their craft smart. The dressing used on the flax sails of a sloop consisted of a mixture of horse fat and ochre.

When sailing, a keel and sloop man's best friend was his anchor. Starting off or stopping, riding with the tide, the skipper steering his vessel with the crown of the anchor just touching the bottom. If there was little or no wind, the anchor cable was hove short until the anchor dropped on the bottom; the vessel could be steered across the tide either way by use of the rudder. Paying out chain stopped the vessel dragging to one side. In a river with strong tides, progress was achieved by dropping the anchor onto the bottom and proceeding stern first. This was known as dredging. A kedge (hawser attached to a small anchor) enabled vessels to be warped (hauled)out of a creek and a dog leg enabled her to moor to a bank.

After reading a report of a motorised barge becoming stranded on a sandbank for two days, Hull-based Sammy Harrison scoffed at their lack of seamanship. Originally from the West Riding, Sammy was mate on a number of keels and sloops. In similar circumstances to those of the motorised barge, he had stood at the bow of a keel and thrown coal down in front of the vessel. The surging tide encountered on the River Humber swirled round the keel and sucked the coal into the mud under the keel's bottom creating a vacuum; soon the keel rocked and sailed off.

When entering a river, some boats would take on an extra hand, known as a purchaseman. This casual worker helped in difficult conditions.

If ever a vessel sprung a leak, the skipper attached a saucepan, filled with sawdust, to a stower and shoved it near the source of the leak. The water sucked the sawdust into the hole; the swelling sawdust filled the hole and plugged it. This technique was known as "branmash".

Other local terms in use:

briggate:-	headroom under a bridge
swill:-	pouring off of water from a sandbank on a falling tide
first of the flood:-	turn of the tide after ebb
hang-on:-	towing
give a pluck:-	hawser to tow off a sandbank
ness:-	sand- or mud-bank at the mouth of a tributary
livering:-	discharging of cargo
went-on:-	aground on a sandbank

Among the many support industries which serviced the keels and sloops were Rayment and Sharp of Hull (ships' chandlers), Brown and Clapson of Barton (ship repairers), W. G. Bingham and Co. of Hull (ships' chandlers), Hall's Ropery of Barton, H. Earles of Hull (sail makers), J. Sinclair of Hull and B. Prissick of Hessle, (both blockmakers).

Watersports were popular features in the life of keel and sloop men and their families, especially in Beverley, Hull, Driffield and Stainforth. Cog boat racing, greasy pole and other aquatic events were keenly contested, sometimes for valuable prizes. The events were usually held on August Bank Holiday Monday.

Fred Holt was mate to his father on the sloop *Sprite* in 1936, having started work on the river as mate under Captain Carter on the sloop *Providence*. His wages were 10/- (50p) per week plus his food provided and he mainly worked the Hull-Gainsborough route.

'Holtie', as he was known on Hull docks where he had worked as a lighterman, won second prize at Hull Music Festival with a poem about an aegir, which was a tidal flood on a river, usually at low water on a spring tide in dry weather with no wind. An aegir (or eagre) occurred on the Humber and the Trent and if the air was still, it could be heard coming ten minutes before its arrival. A keel or sloop would put its head downstream to meet the oncoming waves.

Fred recalled a practical joke played one night at the Friendship Inn at Keadby. Just before closing time, the crews having spent a convivial evening together waiting for the tide to rise and enable them to lock out onto the main river, a couple of bargemen left the pub before the others removed the rudder from one of the keels and hove it up to the top of the mast. When high tide came and the other keels made off, this one had to remain and owing to the darkness, the crew were unable to see their rudder high up on the mast.

Barracloughs of Hull started business as barge owners in 1885. Their first keel was the *Triumph*. Norman Barraclough, whose father and uncle started the business, was barge foreman. He sailed on sloops for over forty years and as a mate his weekly wage was 10/- (50p) plus his food. All this for seven days a week. Trade unions were taboo in his day and he was often away for a fortnight at a time. After twelve successive weekends working, Norman rebelled and refused to sail on another trip. "I was courting and didn't want to lose her." His uncle told him to call and see him in his office on the Monday morning. Norman did so, fully expecting his cards but instead he received a 5/- (25p) a week wage increase.

Norman made many trips up and down rivers and canals and remembers one trip vividly.

> "We had unloaded our cargo in Gainsborough and went to pick up a return cargo of sugar beet from a Lincolnshire farmer. We tied up and called to the farmer who had come up onto the bank to greet us; 'Where's the sugar beet then?' He replied, 'O'er there, under all that watter.' The field was flooded."
>
> "Do you know", chuckled Norman, "we had to wait until the water drained away before we could load up."

With no telephones handy to rely on, the crew often had to send postcards to their employer asking for instructions and await the reply.

In 1939 Barracloughs had fifteen sloops rigged and working up and down the Humber. In fact they owned the last rigged sloop to sail, the *Sprite*, unrigged in 1950 and converted into a lighter. Jack Chant was her skipper. *Sprite* was built by Warrens of New Holland in 1910 for Mark Scott, seedcrushers of Selby and she was 68ft long with a 17ft 6in beam and a deadweight capacity of 165 tons.

Barracloughs also owned the sloop *Ivie* which was originally named *Ivy*, but changed to avoid confusion with another sloop of the same name. *Ivie* was built by Joseph Scarr of Beverley in 1900 and was 65ft long with a deadweight capacity of 140 tons. Several of Barraclough's sloops were converted into powered craft and made regular trips to Gainsborough and inland destinations.

A fully laden sloop *Ivie* with skipper
Tom Chant on the tiller and his son
Ron at the windlass.
R. F. Smith

William Henry Harrison and employees
of one of Beverley's carpenters' yards.
The keel is the *Jane and Maria*, c.1900.
Author's collection

Mr. R. F. Smith of Barton-on-Humber was most helpful during my research in Lincolnshire as well as supplying some interesting photographs and putting me in touch with several ex-skippers, he sent me the following reminiscences:-

"The elements of danger that the sloopmen faced at times is perhaps well illustrated by the following extracts from the collection of newspaper cuttings in my possession.

"In December 1934, Fred Walker and his son George of Barton were the crew of a sailing sloop. They both became ill on a trip out of Hull, George dying later in Scunthorpe hospital. It is thought that fumes given off by her cargo were the cause. Mr. Walker senior recovered but has never been able to work again."

"Two Howden men had narrow escapes last night (20th September 1935) when a sloop floundered in thirty feet of water in the Humber, just off Barton Haven. The sloop Dora, owned by Mr. J. W. Eastwood of Barmby Marsh, was loaded with over sixty tons of chalk from quarries at South Ferriby Sluice and left yesterday for Barmby. When the vessel got into the river it encountered rough waters and a gale of wind. There were two men on board, the skipper Henry Rooke of Barmby Marsh and the mate, William Hutton of Rowland Hall, near Howden. The skipper told a 'Hull Daily Mail' reporter this morning that the ship was soon in difficulties and the foresail was blown away. They immediately dropped anchor and it refused to hold and the vessel dragged down the river towards Hull, completely out of control. Water came aboard in large quantities and the Dora was at the mercy of the tide. When the two men had done all they could, they scrambled onto the cog boat and set off for the shore. After an anxious and dangerous voyage through rough waters, they landed at South Ferriby sluice. Two sloops belonging to the same firm, Brilliant Star and Sunbeam stood by and Brilliant Star eventually managed to get a rope aboard the Dora and took her in tow, dragging her out of the channel on to the Barton sand where she foundered last night about half a mile from Barton waterside."

Mr. Smith lived in houses commanding excellent views of the River Humber for over thirty years. He recalled seeing as many as twelve sloops, under sail and fully laden, in the short reach between Hessle and North Ferriby churches, sometimes making what would seem to be extremely slow progress against the wind. He also told me:

"While I was walking on the river bank near New Holland when the wind was near to gale force, a sloop broke loose from her moorings and was carried broadside down river on a collision course with New Holland Pier. The sloop was only saved from destruction by the strenuous efforts of two men (presumably her crew) who came after her in a dingy and scrambled aboard at what was a considerable physical risk."

Vic Ratcliffe was an apprentice shipwright at Oliver Thompsons of Knottingley in 1911 and joined Richard Dunston's in 1918. His father was licensee of the Roper's Arms Hotel in Knottingley and his uncle, George Draper, sailed on the keels on the Lister Keys to Brigg run. Friends of Vic's would load ash at Knottingley Glass Works and sail down the Aire and Calder Canal to the River Derwent where they unloaded from their keel at two different points on the river bank, returning later to pick up cash from farmers who had taken a load. As Vic recalled, people were a shade more honest in those days.

Captain George Hardy, who was born in East Hull, was captain of the sloop *Brilliant Star* in 1900. The sloop was iron built and carried a jib, foresail, topsail and mainsail. She had a capacity of 90 tons, and worked out of Hull to King's Lynn, Wells, Spalding and Snettisham, usually loaded with cattle cake from BOCM. George had a two-man crew, Albert was mate and Jim was cook-cum-deckhand and the three were a complete team. In 1912 they helped two tugs, the *Swift* and the *Fairy*, to raise another tug, the *Clansman*, which had sunk off Spurn Point with the loss of several crewmen. George would take his wife and small son on some trips; tying a rope around his son's waist, he made it fast to the stern rail and allowed him to steer.

C. B. Colleridge of South Cave had an early baptism when he fell overboard from his father's keel *Hero* at Allerton Bywater when he was only two years old. He was fished out with a boat hook, safe and well and with a lesson learnt. His father later worked another keel, *Perseverance*, and while the tug *Enterprise* was towing her and three other keels from Selby to York, an aegir caused a collision and *Perseverance* was holed. The breach was filled with a flock mattress until they reached York for repairs.

The Keel and Lighter Owners Mutual Insurance and Protecting

Society Ltd., a non-profit making organisation, opened offices in Hull in 1894. They surveyed keels, sloops, ketches and lighters and insured these vessels, their cog boats, leeboards and sails. The maximum insurance was: small boats £7; sails £10 and leeboards £10. The craft themselves were covered for their value, anywhere between £250 and £800. They were surveyed when lying at one of a number of points in Hull, but mainly in the Old Harbour, Queens Dock, St. Andrew's Dock, Fish Dock, Alexandra Dock, Albert Dock, Victoria Dock, Prince's Dock, North Eastern Railway Dock, Hessle Haven, Minerva Pier or Humber Dock.

An entry in the surveyor's report book of 1899 records that the keel *Tiger*, built by Mr. Parkinson Groves of Hull in 1874 and owned by William Sheet, Hull, had a capacity of 90 tons and was 58ft long with a beam of 14ft 10in. In 1899 she cost £110 in repairs and a further £16 in 1903 while 375ft of new planking cost £42. The keel was insured at the time for £150.

Probably the last keel to carry cargoes was the *Nar* of Hull, owned by Furley and Co. and captained by Albert Barrass. The *Nar* was working the Hull-Gainsborough run until 1941 when she was unrigged and converted into a motor powered vessel.

During the Second World War with a need for quick mechanised transport, the British Government gave barge owners grants to convert from sail to power and a great many keels were fitted with 21 hp engines.

The Humber keel declined at a time when it should have been at the height of its glory, in a manner similar to that of the fully rigged sailing ships. The coming of the railways, steam tugs, motor lorries and motorised steel barges all contributed over two decades to the death of the Humber keel as a trading vessel. They were the last square-rigged commercial vessels to survive in British waters, reaching their greatest glory at the end of the 19th century.

Fred Schofield's mother and father on the *Comrade* at Stainforth in 1934. His youngest sister, Winifred, is standing on the hatches and Fred's wife, Lillian is seated beside her.
The Humber Keel and Sloop Preservation Society

The unrigged West Country boat *Thomas Sugden* on the Calder and Hebble Navigation.
The horse marine is Emmanuel Wadsworth, known as "Manny Wanny".
Collection of Hugh McKnight Photography

The canal and inland waterway complex was one of the earliest features of the Industrial Revolution. Coupled with the Agricultural Revolution, it produced an era that demanded quick movement of merchandise and produce from the industrial West Riding of Yorkshire and the agricultural lowlands of Lincolnshire, Nottinghamshire and the vales of the North and East Ridings of Yorkshire. Keels and sloops provided the cheapest and fastest method of movement. Hull was an ideally suited port for exporting, and the river Humber a natural outlet from the waterways of the whole hinterland.

THE AIRE AND CALDER NAVIGATION

The Aire and Calder Navigation was made navigable to the rivers in 1699. The River Aire united with the River Calder at Castleford and continued via Fryston Hall, Ferrybridge, Knottingley, Beal, Haddlesey, Weeland, Snaith and Rawcliffe and turned into the River Ouse at Airmyn, near Howden; a distance of thirty-two miles with ten locks. The Aire was not navigable above Leeds. In 1788, the five mile stretch of canal between Haddlesey and Selby was cut and resulted in Knottingley and Selby replacing York as shipping points. Tolls of ½d per ton per mile were charged and freights limited to 60 tons.

On 20th July 1826, the Knottingley to Goole canal was opened and as a result of this eighteen mile stretch of waterway, which locked out into the River Ouse, an immense amount of trade was brought to Goole, at that time a small village. It quickly grew into a bustling port, outstripping its neighbour Selby, and around £750,000 was spent on the new docks at Goole.

The Aire and Calder Navigation became the most prosperous and efficient waterway in the country and by 1820 shareholders were being paid dividends of 300% per annum. It was certainly the busiest waterway in the area and the amount of traffic using it enabled very low tolls to be charged. From the late 1880s to the early 1900s an average yearly profit of £100,000 was recorded. Coal and wheat were the main cargoes for the Aire and Calder keels. They were slightly different from the Humber keels, having a transom, stern, more decorative poop rails and a pointed bow.

So many craft used the Aire and Calder that it was said that no one ever drowned if they fell into the water; they were poisoned first because of the wool grease and chemical pollution.

When the Selby Canal was being cut, work done mainly by Irish navvies, a horse was reported stolen at Rawcliffe. Police immediately suspected the navvies and they set out for the latter's hostel, having evidence of the man responsible. Warned by the impending arrival of the police, the suspect quietly shaved, donned a woman's nightdress and got into bed. His disguise fooled the authorities and they went away empty-handed.

THE BARNSLEY CANAL

The Royal Assent for this canal to be cut was passed in 1793 and it was opened in June 1799. The canal commenced from the River Calder about a mile below Wakefield Bridge and terminated at Barnby Basin; a distance of fifteen miles, involving twenty locks. The smallest lock was Heath lock, near Wakefield with only six feet of water. Keels entered the lock, one gate was closed and the keel pushed to one side to allow the other gate to be closed. The number of collieries on this stretch of water kept keels in constant work carrying coal through the farms and villages in the Vale of York. Coal was tolled at 1d a ton in 1799.

The new steel keel *Pageant*, built in 1909, the year of the York Pageant, was captained by Captain Colleridge. She ran to Sharlston, West Wallsend and Monk Bretton collieries and could carry 115 tons of coal from Monk Bretton and 122 tons from Sharlston compared to a normal keel's loads of 90 and 100 tons respectively.

Reaching Royston Bridge one fine day, Captain Colleridge found that *Pageant*, unladen, was six inches too high to go under. He and his mate had to bale water into the hold and forecastle to lower her into the water; a task which took a full working day.

On the next journey through, the two o'clock afternoon shift was just leaving the pit and watching Captain Colleridge and his mate once again baling water in. One of the miners asked "What's tha doin' that fer, old lad?" When told the reason, twenty or so miners jumped on board and crowded the forecastle and hold. In ten minutes *Pageant* ran under the bridge with room to spare. After these two incidents Captain Colleridge loaded five tons of coal into the forecastle to lower *Pageant* into the water: it was still there when his employer sold the keel some years later.

The winter of 1912 was a very severe one. At Christmas, the Colleridge family made a trip to Sharlston and became iced up there. Ice breakers were barges up to 40ft long which had long iron bars fitted fore and aft down the centre and carried eight men on each side. They were pulled through by a team of six horses on the towpaths breaking up the ice as they went along. Despite all this help, *Pageant* and several other keels remained iced in. Eventually the pit manager came down to offer help and the pit locomotive was brought along the railway line on top of the coal waste and each keel was towed free. This worked for a distance of about four hundred yards but the ice was so thick that the keels soon became trapped again and it was four weeks before the weather relented and they could leave.

BEVERLEY BECK

Beverley Beck was deepened and widened in 1726 and ran into Beverley from the River Hull at a point practically opposite Weel. The tolls collected on this one mile stretch of water were used solely for keeping the creek tidy, the staithes kept in a state of repair and the upkeep of roads leading to the beck.

Coal was the main cargo brought in by keels and sloops and it was unloaded by the skipper and his mate who rigged a gantry and derrick with two men heaving out of the hold and a fifth man barrowing it away from the wharf to waiting wagons or, in the early 19th century, to the Beverley gasworks. Early records tell of tolls for faggots at 1d per 100 and nails at 4d per 16 bags.

In 1803, a lock was built at the entrance from the River Hull, which meant a constant deep channel of water. The size of keels and sloops which could use the lock was restricted to 65ft in length. Despite its long history, the waterway barely made a profit. Gillyon, Holgate and Peck were familiar names of keelmen on the Beverley Beck.

David Holgate retired from life aboard in 1970 and two years later was still making the ten minute walk from his home to Beverley Beck each morning. His son Edgar skippered the motor-powered barge *Hope* out of Beverley. She had been built at Scarrs of Beverley in 1908 at a cost of £600. At first she had been sloop rigged but was later changed to a keel rig. David's father had been a keelman and his first keel was *Friendship*, in which he had a half share with Tommy Charlton. Although mainly engaged on the coal trade between Keadby and Hull Fish Dock with fuel for the large fleet of coal burning trawlers, David was probably the only man to sail a keel from Hull to Liverpool and back which he managed with a very narrow keel which fitted the many locks en-route. "We went through Foulridge tunnel on the Leeds-Liverpool canal. It was over a mile long and the opening was like a half crown coin in the distance."

Another trip took him from Beverley to Bridlington in the keel *Thomas Scarr* with a 100 ton load of bricks. This keel was later renamed *Ailsa* and was sold to Percy Andrews. David's colleagues in those days included Fred Way, Fudge Tattersall, John Thomas Peck and Alf Shires. David reckoned that a keel, given a fair wind, would always beat a sloop over a distance.

CAISTOR CANAL

Caistor Canal commenced on the River Ancholme near Creampoke and ended at Moortown, a distance of four miles with six locks. The Act for making a navigable canal here was passed in 1793. It enabled the agricultural produce of the area to be conveyed to the ports for redistribution and the keels and sloops brought back coal and lime to the area.

THE CALDER AND HEBBLE NAVIGATION

The Calder and Hebble Navigation opened to commercial traffic in 1758. The locks on this canal were 57ft long and 14ft 2in wide which meant that most keels were too long to use this waterway. First proposals called for twenty-one locks on the Calder and three on the Hebble. Coal from Thornhill Colliery, Dewsbury was the main cargo for the keels; lime, slate, coal and stone were initially charged at 1/1½d (6p) per ton.

DEARNE AND DOVE CANAL

This canal was a nine mile stretch of waterway with eighteen locks which was completed in 1804. It ran from near Swinton to its termination at the junction with the Barnsley Canal via Wath, Brampton, Wombwell and Ardsley. The canal served as an outlet for the numerous coalfields in the area and the coal was of varying grades; slack, smudge, hard and soft coal.

DRIFFIELD CANAL

Driffield Canal received the Royal Assent in 1767 after William Porter, licensee of the Bell Hotel in Driffield, had long championed the cause of a waterway linking isolated Driffield with Hull.

Previous movement of merchandise had been by horse or

The keel *Mary Jane* of Frodingham seen on the Driffield Canal at Frodingham Beck.
Author's collection

mule pack. Kilham was the capital of the East Yorkshire Wolds but when this eleven mile long canal was opened to shipping in 1772 it brought immediate prosperity to Driffield which at that time had a population of 750.

Warehouses were built at River Head and merchant's offices were opened in the town. James Mortimer, Ranks, Bradshaw, Byass and Appleton became increasingly familiar names over the years. Driffield soon replaced Kilham as the "Capital of the Wolds". There were five locks on the Driffield Canal: Aike Beck Mouth to Struncheon Hill (or New Lock) above Beverley, Snakeholme Lock, Wansford Lock, Winnhill Lock and Top Lock. Only keels operated on this canal and became known as Driffield Traders, bringing cargoes of bricks, coal, timber or groceries from Hull, returning with linseed, cotton seed, wheat, soap, oil or wood.

At times up to twenty keels could be seen loading and unloading at River Head. Oil was enclosed in 5cwt steel casks. In a hot afternoon sun, the unloading of coal was warm work and doubtless the nearby Blue Bell public house provided the workers with an excellent reviver. Sworn weighers in Hull weighed the cargo which was then sealed. The captain of the keel presented his bill of lading at the merchant's office after unloading

Keel under full sail at Brigham Swing Bridge on the Driffield Canal.
G. Waites

37

No work was carried out by the quaymen on Saturday afternoon or Sunday.

The thirty mile journey from Hull was once completed by Captain Darwin in the keel *Dauntless* in one day. This was with a favourable wind but in a hard winter a keel could be en-route for up to six weeks. Driffield traders usually carried cargoes of between sixty and seventy tons of coal; the Randall family of Driffield were well-known carriers.

There were no lock keepers at any of the locks and the first toll charges called for 6d (2½p) for every quarter of malt, oats or barley; 6d for every sack of flour; for every cauldron of coal (45 bushels) the charges were 3/6d (17½p) which was reduced to 9d (4p) in 1898. The tow path rate from Hull Bridge to Fisholme Corps Landing and Frodingham was ½d per ton per mile.

Despite its importance to Driffield in trading movement, the canal was not commercially viable. In 1888, with a tonnage of 29,000, there was a profit of £98; in 1898 tonnage carried 24,000 with a loss of £37; in 1905 with a tonnage of 33,000 a profit of just £13. Richardson, Porter, Butterworth, Darwin, Verity and Hought were some of the well-known keel families on the waterway.

Mrs. D. A. Darwin sailed with her husband on the keels *Priscilla* and *William* between 1910 and 1922. During the winter the Darwins and their family sailed from Driffield to Hull with general cargoes while in the summer they carried timber to Huddersfield, wire to Halifax and wheat to Sowerby Bridge and brought back coal from Monkton or Monk Bretton to Hull Fish Dock. Their Driffield cargoes included cotton seed or linseed from Hull to the Driffield Cake Company and they returned with oil for Barker Lee Smith. In 1926 Captain Darwin bought the keel *Chrysoidine* and brought down corn for E. B. Bradshaw of Driffield. Mrs. Darwin would often haul the keel along with a long rope connected to a post on board and with a canvas covering on her shoulders, she would pull the keel along, especially if there was no wind. It was known as "bow yankin" and Mrs. Darwin was once asked by a landlubber if it was hard work. She replied "No, you just pull and it follows." When they reached Brigham swing bridge, Bradshaw's would have a man waiting with a horse to tow them the remainder of the way to Driffield. In 1935 *Chrysoidine* was converted to power at Thorne but Captain Darwin kept the sail for emergencies as these often arose when reeds along the river bank became entangled in the propeller. "It was a hard life but a good one", Mrs. Darwin told me. E. B. Bradshaw owned three keels which sailed regularly until 1940 with cargoes of corn. The canal became virtually impassable in 1942.

FOSS NAVIGATION

The twelve mile long navigation began at New Inn, Sheriff Hutton Bridge and continued by Strensall, Towthorpe, Earswick and Huttington to York and flowed into the River Ouse.

FOSSDYKE NAVIGATION

This very ancient canal dating from Roman times was eleven miles long and started at Torksey on the River Trent and was joined by the River Witham at Lincoln before the River Till fell into it. Keels and sloops played an important part in local life by bringing coal to the area. A trip from Lincoln to Hull averaged twelve hours and two trips a month was considered good. The 1914 river dues were usually 8d (4p) per ton.

A very shallow draught was encountered on this waterway and in 1921 a Captain Smith spent nine days at Torksey lock waiting for a 5ft draught. From here the journey to Lincoln was via Long Wrack, Drinsey Nook, Saxilby Bridge, Brayford, High Bridge, Thorn Bridge and Co-op Mill. A very peaceful calm canal in pleasant countryside.

In 1833, the engineer Isambard Kingdom Brunel surveyed the waterway at the invitation of the proprietors following complaints about its condition by boat owners. After inspecting keels on Brayford Mere, he journed from Torksey to Lincoln on the laden keel *Industry* which was pulled by two horses. The journey was uneventful until they came to the high bridge on the River Witham; *Industry* became stuck in the mud and had to be warped along.

Two keels along the Lincoln Road, near Saxilby on the Fossdyke Canal, 1922.
M. L. Mann

One of the last keels seen on the ancient Fossdyke Canal en-route for Torksey via Drinsey Nook on the Gainsborough Road, 1941.
A. L. Mann

A keel in full sail near Burton Lane End on the ancient Fossdyke Canal, 1922.
M. L. Mann

GRIMSBY HAVEN

This large cut connected Grimsby with the River Humber and was opened in 1800. The waterway was 1½ miles long and had one lock. John Frank of South Ferriby was owner/master of a keel working to Louth and the lower Humber. Captain Frank's keel mainly carried cargoes of bricks from the brickyards of North Lincolnshire to Grimsby and in 1922 carried a total of 2,075,500 bricks. With sails tied up, leeboards lowered onto the river bed to keep the boat steady, a plank was lowered from quay to keel and the bricks were barrowed aboard, fifty at a time. Three men wheeled and one stowed. In this way 4,000 bricks could be loaded aboard in an hour. Leaving the brickyard at South Ferriby, Horkstow or Burton Stather, Captain Frank sailed past Barton, Barrow-on-Haven, New Holland pier, Goxhill Haven, cleared Skitter Ness and Whitebooth Roads with spray flying into the sails, reached Holm Side followed by Killingholme Haven, past the monument to the Pilgrim Fathers who sailed from Immingham Dock, inside Burcum Sand and then on to unload at Grimsby. He and his mate threw off three bricks at a time, four men stacking the bricks on the quayside. The discharging took about eight hours; Captain Frank usually returned to Hull with a cargo of timber, pit props or matches.

John Frank's favourite bridge was Keadby Bridge; "a good bridge to run under", while he considered cattle to be his most difficult cargo. He took them from South Ferriby to Selby, Brough, Hessle or Reads Island (also known as Old Warp) for grazing, but they were difficult to stow. "They would all move from one side of the hold to the other and it was a devil of a job to bring the keel about". John Frank had a passionate interest in the days of sail and once he worked two keels on one tide. He would be off to Hull, unload, and then catch the steam ferry from Hull to New Holland and take out a second keel on the next tide. He continued doing this until he was obliged to stop owing to ill health caused by over-work.

He remembered the sloop *Masterman* sinking off Whitton Ness in the Humber in 1910 with the loss of three lives and the keel *Marley Hill* foundering off Whitton Ness. She remained buried for years and was then washed out after which she was raised, re-rigged and sailed again.

In 1907 Joe Waddington was skipper when *Nero* was hit by the steam keel *Gwynwal* off Swinefleet and Joe was drowned. His body was picked up ten days later at Hook. History repeated itself in 1937 when Joe's son Henry was knocked overboard from the same sloop in Hull Roads and he was also drowned.

John Frank had a hard working life, and knew the art of mooring at Hall's, Stoneferry, Horseferry, Reckitt's and Houlton wharves in Hull and Markham's wharf in Grimsby, he was an expert in the art of sailing and handling his craft and the quickest way of handling cargoes on and off a keel or sloop.

Keels viewed from Magpie Bridge
(now Thorne Bridge), Lincoln,
waiting to load at Lincoln Cake Mill in 1910.
W. E. R. Hallgarth

HEDON HAVEN

The ancient harbour of Hedon was improved in 1774 and was regularly used by Humber keels and sloops. The first tolls charged 3/6d (17½p) for every cauldron of coal while every quarter of wheat, rye, beans, peas or rape seed cost 6d (2½p).

LEVEN CANAL

Mrs. Charlotte Bethel of Rise financed this three mile long canal which was opened in 1801. It started near Aike Beck mouth on the River Hull and enabled supplies of coal, lime and manure to be brought to Leven and provided an outlet for the surrounding district to send its corn and agricultural produce to Hull and Beverley. In 1805 a toll rate of 7/- (35p) for every boat or barge using the canal was introduced. Maxwell's warehouse was at the terminal basin, and Turnbull's Coal Merchants had a coal bunker on the bank. The canal was closed to commercial traffic in 1936.

LOUTH CANAL

Louth canal opened in the late 18th century and was considerably improved in 1828. It was fourteen miles long and ran from Tetney Haven to Alvington and then on to Louth.

Keels awaiting loading
on the River Ancholme at Brigg Bridge.
Scunthorpe Museum

A sloop entering Tetney Lock on the Louth Canal in 1910.   *W. E. R. Hallgarth*

MARKET WEIGHTON CANAL

Starting at New River Head close to Market Weighton it ran for eleven miles with four locks via Everingham, Seaton Ross, Holme-upon-Spalding Moor, Foggathorp and Fossdyke Clough, locking out into the River Humber near Newport. The canal opened in 1775 and this very straight stretch of water enabled some of the fastest sloops to sail on it. A stone set in the bridge near the Humber lock gates records that the lock was repaired in 1826 by Mr. Grundy, engineer; Mr. Allen, surveyor; Mr. Smith, carpenter; and Mr. Jefferson, mason. Early tolls of 4/- (20p) a ton for groceries, 1/- (5p) a ton for stone, 6d (2½p) per 1000, for bricks are noted.

POCKLINGTON CANAL

This was an inland navigation, nine miles long, originally with four locks, later extended to nine. Leaving the River Derwent, the waterway stretched from East Cottingwith to Street Bridge in Pocklington. Coal and lime were brought into the area and corn was shipped out. Cut under an Act of 1815, the canal was opened in 1818.

RIVER ANCHOLME NAVIGATION

Opening at the Ferriby sluice on the River Humber it ran for fourteen miles before it reached the Caistor canal. Completed in 1767, there were only two locks. Bricks and tiles were charged at a toll fee of 1/8d (9p per thousand, amended in 1802 to 4d (2p) per thousand. The lock charge was 2/6d (12½p) in 1901.

RIVER DERWENT

The Derwent, which falls into the Ouse at Barmby-on-the-Marsh, was navigable for small barges for fifty miles up to Yedingham Bridge, with locks at Stamford Bridge, Buttercrambe, Howsham, Kirkham Abbey and Sutton-on-Derwent. It is recorded that during the last decade of the 19th century, two sloops were engaged to trade on the river. It was a very useful river, enabling coal to be brought to the many hamlets on its banks and the area's extensive wheat crops to be transported to the West Riding. It was probably the only river which had a towpath specifically constructed for horses to pull the barges. Very difficult to navigate, nevertheless the Derwent provided an easier mode of transport than the bad roads of the 18th and early 19th centuries. Keels using the river Derwent were termed "West Country Boats" and were 55ft long and 14ft wide.

The Haven at Barton Waterside, a shallow tidal waterway which linked the town
with inland ports via the River Humber
Grimsby Central Library

RIVER HULL

The quays and wharves were very numerous at Hull and the river was always busy with keels and sloops sailing up and down, to and from the Wolds and out into the River Humber and beyond.

RIVER HUMBER

This major river was the ultimate destination of most keels and sloops. The import and export trade through Hull meant a steady living for the rivermen plying to and from wharves on the estuary. The treacherous sandbanks of the Humber meant great care had to be taken in navigating. By the middle of the 19th century, tugs began helping shipping, saving time and money by towing four or five vessels together to Keadby or Goole at around 10/- (50p) each. Bob Cooper's *Hydro, Swift, Fairy, Sir Joseph Rhymer* (York), *Ebie*, the 50hp *Britannia* and the steam keels *Ouse* and *Gwynwaul* were all seen in regular work on the Humber.

Large ships were saved paying port dues by an Act of Parliament which enabled them to unload their cargoes over the sides to the waiting keels and sloops below.

A keel being poled along at Arram on the River Hull, c.1936.
Author's collection

A sloop in this busy shipping scene on the River Humber.
Hull Daily Mail

Mr. W. A. King-Webster of Garlieston, Scotland, wrote to me in the 1970s regarding his memories of keels and sloops.

"The following notes will contain nothing new to you if you have spent your life near the Humber and are late middle-aged like myself. If however, you are younger, they may be of some interest, as they refer to the last few years of commercial sail.

*"I was apprenticed to a shore job in Hull in 1943 and on landing from the New Holland ferry, saw my first sloop tied up immediately down river from the ferry landing. Being already deeply interested in inshore sailing craft, I took the first opportunity of making the acquaintance of her skipper and subsequently made several trips in this vessel **Ever Ready** and her sister ships.*

*"She was one of three 62ft sloops belonging to a family called Stamp and they carried general cargo between Hull and Barton-on-Humber. The other two were called **Rising Hope** and **Rosalie Stamp**. They were old-fashioned wooden sloops with a large main hatch abaft the mast and a small fore-hatch forward. I will not describe them further as you must have*

The keel *Mary Jane* sailing up the River Hull under mainsail, topsail and topgallant. Owned by Captain Bob Wood, she was built in 1882.
Fred Schofield

access to plans and photographs.

*"I cannot remember the skipper's name but he was an old man who had stayed on owing to the war. His son skippered the 69ft **Burgate**, a sloop of similar layout and construction but impressively larger. They were a very likeable family and proud of their seamanship.*

"The Barton run was a routine affair. Cargo was loaded or discharged by derrick and hand-wound dolly winch except for packages light enough to be tossed from hand to hand. Then, on the same tide, one sloop left Hull as soon as she floated on the flood which she rode up to Barton, while another sloop left Barton at high water and took the first of the ebb down to Hull. It was thus able to make the two-way trip in a few hours.

"I was greatly impressed by the sloop's efficiency under Humber conditions. No small sailing craft could hope regularly to stem the powerful tides, while travelling with the tide at a satisfactory speed. Speed through the water therefore could be sacrificed to cargo capacity which resulted in a hull-form as near that of an oblong box as possible. With tides to help her, a sloop's sail plan could be as basic and as

Zurial, a West Country keel, on the River Hull at Hull Bridge Mills near Beverley.
H. L. Cartlidge

economical as possible; the bob-tailed gaff mainsail and foresail achieved this. To give some manoeuvrability and lateral resistance without reducing cargo capacity, a pair of leeboards were the obvious answer.

"For some time I wondered whether a sloop could, in fact, work to windward when light without a tide under her. However, I later saw one cast off from the eastern end of one of the larger docks and beat up to the lock pits against a lightish westerly breeze. One could see the broad slick as her empty hull made leeway despite the resistance of her board, nevertheless she gained an impressive amount of ground to windward each tack. The skipper of the **Ever Ready** told me that it did not pay to pinch a sloop to windward with the boom-end inside the lee coaming of the hatch. To have done so would have back-winded the foresail in any case as its leech was laced to the forward shroud on each tack, which made it far from close-winded.

"While on the subject of sloop's efficiency as a cargo carrier under Humber conditions, I should perhaps mention the deck layout of the last vessels to be built. These were of iron or steel and had the same continuous hatch extending the length of the hold as had a keel, the halyard and topping-lift winches being abeam of the mast at the foot of the shrouds. This greatly facilitated loading and unloading bulk cargoes with modern equipment.

"There is little I can say about the handling of the sloops under sail which you will not already know. Most of the trips I made were in moderate to light winds, in which they stayed quite readily, the mate keeping the foresail backed until the bow was well through the wind when he let go the rope lacing the bottom of the leech to the forward shroud on the weather side and laced it in again to the lee shroud. The skipper of the **Ever ready** told me that most sloops sailed and handled best when trimmed slightly down by the head. He also told me that in years gone by, sloops had a bowsprit, topsail and a boom extending to the taffrail. In those days they made coastal passages outside the Humber. This story fits well with the appearance of the latter day sloops if one visualises a couple of cloths removed from the leech of the mainsail to balance the loss of the jib and and the reduced mainsail cut higher in the peak, so as to set better close hauled in the absence of a topsail.

Laden sloop on the River Humber c.1932.
Owners were Andertons of Howdendyke, near Goole.
Author's Collection

"I made one trip in quite heavy weather with a westerly gale meeting the last of a spring flood. **Ever Ready** was loaded well short of capacity and rode the considerable seas very dryly with nothing coming on board save a little spray over the bows. The mainsail she had was really too small for her so she had only one or two reefs down, under which sail she stood up well and stayed quite readily on the south side of the Humber. After the return tack, however, she missed stays off St. Andrew's Dock in a sea big enough to toss her about like a dingy. We were too near the stone embankment to try again, so had to gybe her round immediately. The manoeuvre was made more difficult by the fact that the gybe had to be more or less all-standing. As the boom flicked across, the skipper managed to gain a foot or two of sheet and catch a turn on the cleat. Although the rope was springy coir, the jar, as it came taut, shook the ship and made the mast whip while the sheet surged round the cleat.

The skipper had rigged a tiller line in anticipation, without which the kick of the helm could have thrown him overboard. I was told that some skippers streamed the main sheet astern while gybing in any weight of wind to save the risk of a flying turn catching anyone. Gybing was by far the most hazardous manoeuvre with sloop rig, many lives having been lost in the past due to losing control of main sheet or tiller. It also accounted for many broken bones.

"None of my trips were made in a flat calm but I was told that it was possible to dredge across from Hull to Barton with the anchor just dragging on the bottom. Off Barton, the anchor was allowed to hold while the line from the dolly winch was taken ashore in the small boat.

"There were quite a number of other sloops still under sail when I was in Hull. A small fleet of, I think, three big iron ones, used to bring clay from a pit between New Holland and Barton to the mouth of the River Hull where they tied up on the east side to await the next flood on which they rode to some destination up river. Viewed from the St. Andrew's Dock wall, they made a stirring sight as they came foaming down the Humber before a strong westerly wind. One saw quite a few others in the docks, awaiting loading or discharging.

"Keels under sail were a good deal fewer than sloops and I only once saw one with her sail set and that when she was also in tow. What I was most struck by was the way in which the yard swayed about on its mast parrel, in the absence of lifts. Some of those in the dock were still rigged to set a topsail but others were stumped-masted for mainsail only."

Reg Barraclough worked for James Barraclough's of Hull. Captain of the sloop *Annie Maud* out of Barton he often carried chalk cargoes along the Humber to Spurn in the 1930s. The chalk was used to build a wall, strengthening the river bank from Spurn to Kilnsea. Once, when he was blown onshore off Spurn Point with no tide high enough to refloat his sloop, Reg rang the owners who told him to wait for a high tide. This he did, bringing his wife from Barton on the ferry to Hull and then on to Spurn by bus to join him. The 'holiday' lasted for two weeks before there was sufficient high water to refloat his sloop. Reg carried varied cargoes but mostly chalk, wheat, coal and bricks.

A keel off the loading stage at South Ferriby Cliff,
jury rigged with a stump mast.
R. F. Smith

A keel under tow on the River Humber in 1938.
R. F. Smith

'Yorky' Vause was mate on the sloop *Active* out of Barton, working for Aldridges under skipper Ron Jennison. Wages and conditions were very grim. "Mind you", said Yorky, "the owner would always lend you a sub."

Walt Seddon and Joe Wood from Barton-on-Humber both worked for Earle's Cement for a period of forty years. Earle's owned eight sloops, among them *Britannia, Miss Madeline* and *Swinefleet* and they brought clay from Barton across the River Humber and up the River Hull to the cement works at Wilmington. This area would often seem like winter in summer with an almost permanent white dust covering the area. Both Joe and Walt remembered the early days when they had to shovel the clay which fetched around 1/3d (6p) a ton. The

journey from Barton to Wilmington and back took four tides. The mast had to be lowered and the sloop floated on the tide up the River Hull, driving with the anchor and pushed clear of the banks by long poles. When Earle's converted their boats to power, in the mid-1940s, Joe and Walt were both glad and sorry at the same time. Glad, because power meant regular hours could be worked, without reliance on winds and tides and because it also meant they received a regular weekly wage instead of the 'thirds' system of payment previously used. Sorry, because it was the end of an era, harder perhaps to leave because both had known no other method than sail during their working lifetime.

Keels at Barton-on-Humber, 1892.
Collection of Hugh MacKnight Photography

A sloop off 'The Pier, Kingston-upon-Hull' by Thomas J. Sommerscales.
Ferens Art Gallery

Fred Chapman, another Bartonian, worked on sloops for J. Barraclough, Aldridges and Earle's Cement. "It was a hard life, anywhere, anytime; night or day. Always the worry of no work — no pay." Fred began work on sloops in 1901.

Stainforth. There were eleven locks. The canal was improved six times between 1726 and 1826 and effectively served a busy manufacturing area. In 1764, a sixty ton keel, built in 1760, was advertised for sale.

RIVER DON NAVIGATION

This navigation began near Tinsley and flowed eighteen miles, eventually linking up with the Stainforth and Keadby Canal at

RIVER OUSE

This river served York very well until, over the years, it silted up badly. By reason of its easy access to the Humber, the River

Ouse realised its great potential and importance. Keels often used a top gallant (three sails) on blanketed parts to catch the wind above the high trees.

In 1834, Acaster Selby shoal measured over two miles. Keelmen using the river regularly developed infinite patience over the years. Being stranded on a sandbank, or 'neaped' as it was known, meant that a lot of their time was spent high and dry on board, especially at low water in a summer, and they had to wait for a tide of sufficient water to float them off. Some 150 keels were working regularly to York in 1906, but this was reduced to 70 by 1912 and by the 1930s it was an unusual sight to see a fully rigged keel.

On a trip along the Ouse, this time in the summer, the *Pageant* lost one of the flukes off her anchor when it caught the chain of a dredger's mooring line on the bottom of the river near Naburn lock. Despite turning into the side, the keel was eventually brought to.

On one occasion, a steam tug towed four keels with a combined cargo of 3,164 quarters of grain from Hull to York in under ten hours.

Laden keels under tow on the River Trent.
E. W. Carter Collection, Gainsborough Public Library

RIVER TRENT

The River Trent commenced at Trent Falls with the junction of the River Ouse from the River Humber opposite Faxfleet and reached up to Gainsborough via Burton Stather, Keadby, Burringham, West Butterwick, Susworth, Owston Ferry, Wildsworth, Gunthorpe and West Stockwith. An immense area of Yorkshire, Lincolnshire and Nottinghamshire was covered by canals running off this river. The dues in 1914 were 1½d per ton. A penny thrown ashore at locks and bridges ensured a keel could sail through without stopping, thanks to the lock keeper and the bridge man.

In 1704, the sloop *Speedwell* of Gainsborough under Robert Gleadall, carried a cargo for Furley and Co. of Hull. The bill of lading was for 3,400 scythe stones, 4 lasts of malt and 3 tuns of beer. The whole cargo probably only weighed 5 tons.

A variation of the Humber keel and sloop only encountered in the River Trent area was the Lincoln catch or ketch which was 64ft long, sharp at bow and stern with a very shallow draught.

On 1st August 1917, an aegir swept through Owston Ferry, drowning the ferryman, his housekeeper and a servant girl from the local inn.

Lincolnshire was the home of the sloop captain. Chick Chant, Tom Matthews, G. W. Burkill and Alfred Holman were other

Keels meeting an aegir stern-on on the River Trent.
George Brocklehurst Collection, Gainsborough Library

49

well-known skippers all from Barton-on-Humber and engaged in the river trade.

Tommy Newton, Wallis Peck, Bill Newton, Charlie Waterhand, Sammy St. Paul, Charlie Johnson, John Matthews, John Foster, Arthur Foster, Charlie East, Harry Horsefell, Harry Hodgson, Bill Greasey, Wallace Walker, Tom Walker, John Richmond, George Wilson, Dick Harness and Fred Richardson were all masters of sloops sailing the Lincolnshire waterways in the early part of the century.

In an account book of Richard Todd of Owston Ferry, an entry dated October 1906 records a cargo of potatoes sent to E. Bedforth of Humber Street, Hull and invoices at £2.5s.0d (£2.25p) a ton.

An unfortunate accident happened one day at Gunness, when during the unloading of a vessel onto a wagon, the horse and cart both tumbled off the quay into the hold.

A term originating with Trentmen was a 'Charlie Simmser', which meant a smartened up sloop, so called after a Charlie Simms who was so boat proud, he would even wash out his empty coal bunker before it was refilled.

Jack Smith of Lincoln, owned the keel *Vixen* which carried loose wheat from the King George Dock silo in Hull to Lincoln during the early 1940s; one of the last keels to make the run under sail. The *Vixen* was captained by Mr. Cawthorne.

A keel off Keadby Bridge on the River Trent. — *National Maritime Museum, London*

A laden and an unladen keel pass on the River Trent, 1920.
W. E. R. Hallgarth

SHEFFIELD CANAL

Also known as the South Yorkshire Navigation, the Sheffield Canal received the Royal Assent to be cut in 1815. It was four miles long with twelve locks and was the second busiest canal for keels. The waterway connected Sheffield with the River Don and the keels which only used this stretch of canal were painted dark blue.

When a keel was bound for Sheffield out of Hull in the late 19th century, she would be towed by tug to Keadby on the Trent and then hope to get a north-easterly or easterly wind on the Stainforth and Keadby Canal, when she would be under sail. After 1866, when railway bridges were built over the canal, leeboards were shipped ashore at a point near Thorne's low railway bridge and the mast and sails were taken off by hand crane at Mexborough and left in a field on large trestles. This had

to be done because of the many bridges en-route. A large anchor was then taken on board along with some heavy warp. From Stainforth, a 'horse marine', a man who earned his living by hiring out a horse and his services, was engaged for the journey to Sheffield via Doncaster.

Just before 1900, the tug *Ebie* began operations, towing up to five keels at a time. The cost of horse or tug towing was about the same, usually 10/- (50p) a stage, each lock being counted as a stage. However, a horse could only manage a speed of about two miles an hour, so tugs became very popular.

Herbert Wilson was skipper of the keel *Ada Dews* in 1913 when he was 18. The keel had been built at York for use by Henry Leetham's Flour Mills of York and carried coal (the most common cargo on the canal) and flour. Herbert's father, George, had bought the keel *British Oak* from Furleys for £50

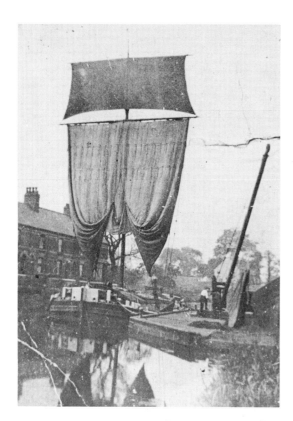

A keel en route for Sheffield having her leeboards removed by hand crane at Thorne. She would be towed from this point and collect her leeboards on the return journey.
Author's Collection

A keel underway on the Sheffield and South Yorkshire Navigation near to Sprotbrough Bridge.
Author's Collection

The keel *Ino* approaching Sprotbrough Lock on the Sheffield and South Yorkshire Navigation.
Author's Collection

and Herbert's brother owned the keel *Lily* at the same time. *Lily* was built by Guests of Mexborough and was eventually sold to Graingers of York for lightering duties.

At Pottery Bridge, with mast lowered and a light cargo aboard, a wily skipper would persuade twenty or so children to come on board and their combined weight would enable the keel to be eased along under the bridge.

STAINFORTH AND KEADBY CANAL

This canal was fifteen miles long and used only one lock, near Thorne. By connecting the Don and Trent rivers it avoided the lower part of the Don. Completed in the late 18th century, this canal was equally popular with keels and sloops and once again, coal was the main cargo carried.

Thorne and Stainforth were centres for keelmen's families:

Schofield, Kaye, Parish, Wilson, Hinchcliffe and Holt were well-known and respected names. During 1903, an average of sixty fully-laden keels passed down through Thorne lock to Keadby.

Alfred Parish bought a new wooden keel, *United*, in 1906 from Thomas Pendlebury of Park Gate Yard near Rotherham. It cost £360 and he paid a deposit of £50 on placing the order, a further £100 during construction and a final £200 on completion, receiving a credit of £10 for his old keel *Johanna*.

Worfolk and Co., boat builders and repairers, of the boat yard in Stainforth, sent an account to Walter Parish for his keel *Edith Annie*. The bill, dated September 1921, was for £78.5s.3d. (£78.26p) and during the three weeks it took to finish the re-caulking and new planking, 446½ hours of men's time was accounted for at a cost of £44.14s.3d. (£44.71p); an hourly rate of 1/11d (9p).

The unladen keel, *Mayday* on the canal at Keadby c.1920. *Author's Collection*

53

Bill Dean once sailed from Doncaster to Hull via this canal in only 16 hours. Billy Foster, captain of *Daybreak* found himself frozen in on this stretch one winter.

Joshua Turner of Barugh Locks near Barnsley built the keel *Fanny* in May 1866 for Henry Pauling, a Hull shipping agent. Her height amidships to the top of the gunwale was 6ft 6in. Clencher built of English oak, with coamings and headledges of American oak and decks of memel redwood, the keel's capacity was 102 tons, decks awash. *Fanny* was 55½ft on keel, 57½ft overall; 6ft 4in skin, 14ft 8in beam and her carval bottom was 2½in thick. The cost of the keel was £290, with the hull of the old keel *Fanny and Rebecca* taken in part exchange. Payment was in stages following the usual practice: £50 when building started, £50 when timbered and the balance on completion and delivery.

In January 1877, John Christopher Schofield of Stainforth bought a half share in *Fanny* for £180. His son, William Henry Schofield of Fishlake, bought the other half share for £50 in July 1892 from Arthur and George Pauling of Hull. William bought out his father in 1900 and sold the keel complete to his brother Arthur in 1904. Arthur, in turn, sold her to Ellis Naylor of Thorne in 1911 and bought her back again in 1920, selling her the same week to William Caldicott of Butterwick. Mr. Caldicott altered the keel to a sloop rig and used her as a weekly market boat between Butterwick, Owston Ferry, Keadby, Crowle Wharfe and Hull. He sold *Fanny* to Captain Abby in 1935, when she was converted to motor power. *Fanny* foundered in an easterly gale in Hull Roads in the winter of 1938. She was raised and broken up on Sammy's Point, Hull. Her working life spanned 71 years.

John Christopher Schofield bought a half share in the keel *Integrity* for £150 in 1911 from his son, William Henry. The keel was worked on the third principle. John took two thirds of the cargo price and paid all expenses while William took one third and the £150 was paid off at 5% interest.

An agreement in May 1891 between J. S. Schofield and Furley and Co. (river and canal carriers and forwarding agents of Hull) recorded that Furleys would pay £50 per annum, to be paid quarterly, to Captain Schofield. The keel was worked on the thirds system, but the owner's third was paid to the hirers. Six days a year were allowed for repair and Captain Schofield was bound over not to become drunk or incapable in charge of his keel. The agreement was witnessed by Fred Baker.

The keel *Guidance*, owned by William Henry Schofield, was registered as a dwelling boat. Under the Canal Boat Act of 1874, amended in 1877, local authorities had to register all canal boats. The boats were all numbered and the number of persons

Billy Foster and his keel *Daybreak* frozen in at Keadby.
Author's Collection

permitted to live on board was fixed: two adults and four children under the age of twelve in the after cabin; two adults and one child in the fore cabin; 60 cubic ft. of free air space for each person under twelve.

Education of the children was a problem. Some attended school one week in three when the keel or sloop trip was finished. Others received no schooling at all. The phrase 'water gypsies' soon stuck to a keelman's family living aboard.

Guidance was completely fitted out in 1905 by Richard Dunston's, shipbuilders and general merchants of Thorne, at a cost of £136.18s.6d (£136.92p). Among the items were:-

Mast (48ft x 10in) at	£ 6.18s.8½d	(£6.94p)
9 yds mainsail and 10ft topsail at	£15.19s.0d	(£15.95p)
wire rigging at	£ 6.13s.2½d	(£6.67p)
ironwork at	14s.1d	(70p)
ropes at	£ 1. 0s.6½d	(£1.02p)
chains at	8s.7½d	(43p).

By 1926 the price of a main sail had risen to £26 compared with £10.16s.2d. (£10.81p) in 1846: a new mast in 1846 had cost £3.

Walter Parish's wife kept an account of her husband's freights on the keel *Edith Annie* based at Stainforth. During the period April 1924 to March 1925 freights were £244.19s.0d. (£244.95p): expenses of £155.11s.5d. left a profit of £129.7s.7d. (£129.38p). The towing charge by tug from Keadby to Hull was listed as 25/-(£1.25p) and the insurance premium for the keel was £3 per quarter. From April 1925 to April 1926 freights were £220.9s.0d (£220.45p), expenses at £140.8s.11d leaving a profit of £80.0s.1d. In 1926, the year of the General Strike, *Edith Annie* was laid up at Kilnhurst Colliery for thirteen weeks and then it took another three weeks for her skipper to find a cargo.

Lionel White was born at Thorne in 1895 and started work on his father's keel *Involvo* which had been built at Scarrs of Grovehill, Beverley, in 1901. Lionel's father had originally owned the keel *Titus*. In 1914 the Government purchased *Involvo* for use on the French waterways during the First World war. Lionel sailed the Hull to Sheffield route, later switching to the Hull to Gainsborough journey. He had chosen to work on a keel as part of a family tradition.

He told me that a captain and his crew were largely self-sufficient but they were also part of a close-knit community. His last trip under sail was in 1930 on the steel keel *William and Annie* which had also been built by Scarrs of Beverley (in 1921 at a cost of £950 cash). "Harnessing the elements was hard work", recalled Lionel, "and although it was enjoyable work for the most part I had no feeling of sorrow at the loss of sail. Diesel craft with their power and covered cabin were comforts I was glad to welcome."

Lionel told me of an incident when he tied up at Hull Docks with a full load, checked the moorings and went off home. When the tide fell, his keel settled through the mud and became fast in the clay underneath. When the tide rose, his keel was stuck tight and water covered her over. He was certainly surprised when he came back next morning and he and his mate had to unload part of their cargo onto another keel before their own keel could be freed. He learnt by this experience and on future occasions he pulled chains round and underneath the keel. Pulling on these chains created a vacuum under the vessel, enabling air to pass through. This operation was known as 'sucking a keel clear'.

RIVER WHARFE

This river was used to ship malt and yeast to the breweries in Tadcaster, the return journey being made with barrels of beer for the countryside pubs. In 1753, Robert Fretweel advertised his services:

"...a number of good closed-decked keels between Hull and Tadcaster and connecting with covered wagons thence to Leeds."

The keel *Willie* of Driffield.
Captain W. Verity, 1895.
Oil by Reuben Chappell.
*National Maritime Museum,
London*

The keel *Ceres* of Saxilby.
Captain W. Binks. Oil by
Reuben Chappell.
Scunthorpe Museum

During the 19th century Hull had a fine reputation for a continuing school of marine painters but, without exception, these artists tended to ignore keels and sloops as subjects. only John Ward featured them regularly in his paintings and then it was usually only half of the vessel. Schooners, whalers, ketches and steam packets were all greater attractions to the marine artist.

However, thirty miles downriver, at Goole, there was an artist who was to sketch and paint pictures of Humber keels and sloops in profusion. His name was Reuben Chappell.

Born at Hook on 21st July 1870, he was the youngest of six children of a joiner who later became a master cabinet maker. Reuben suffered from bronchial weakness early in his life but he still managed to study and won a scholarship to Goole Grammar School which was then privately run. At school he developed an interest in photography and drawing. To encourage his obvious ability, Reuben's father built him a studio at 7, Jackson Street, Goole. It was here that he began his painting career in earnest. Chappell would invite commissions from the many seamen who used the port of Goole, charging 5/-(25p) for a transparent water colour or £1.10s.0d. (£1.50p) for an oil painting. He earned his living selling his paintings and his output was prolific, very often he had to finish a work before the ship departed on the next high tide.

He was very detailed and accurate in his drawings and paintings, using clear, bright colours. His work reflected all types of shipping and his paintings of keels and sloops were with a broadside view, usually off Spurn Point or Whitton Ness on the River Humber, with another ship of the same period added in the corner. He signed his early work 'R. Chappell, Goole' along with the name of the keel or sloop and the name of the captain.

Chappell married Caroline Bayford of Thorne in 1895 and they had three sons. By 1904 his bronchial weakness had become much worse and his doctor advised him to leave the area of cold easterly winds; he moved to the better climate of Par, Cornwall. His wife died there in 1930 and he remarried in 1933. When he died in 1940, Chappell was buried in Fowey cemetery. During his lifetime it was estimated that he had produced over 12,000 paintings. Basil Greenhill, Director of the National Maritime Museum, first brought his work to prominence in the art world and exhibitions of Reuben Chappell's work have been held at

Reuben Chappell, pictured at Par, Cornwall.
National Maritime Museum

The sloop *Lilian* of Hull, with a bowsprit.
The Garside Collection, Goole

The sloop *Ethel* of Hull, with a bowsprit,
off Goole. Captain A. Matthew, c.1910.
The Garside Collection, Goole

galleries in London, Bristol, Goole, Scunthorpe and Doncaster: many of his paintings are on permanent display at Goole Library Museum and Art Gallery. Descendants of seafaring families all over the world are now finding that their Reuben Chappell paintings have an enhanced value as his popularity increases with time.

The sloop *Mafeking* of Barton built by Brown and Clapson in May 1900.
Captain T. Barraclough. Oil by Reuben Chappell.
R. Clapson

The keel *Mayday* lying rotting in a timber pond at Goole, 1968.
Hull Daily Mail

The Humber Keel Trust was formed in 1952 under the patronage of the Lord Mayor of Hull, Alderman H. Jacobs. The Chairman of the trust was Mr. Kenneth Grimes.

The object of the Trust was to acquire at least one specimen of the Humber Keel under sail. The idea of a keel, with a permanent static berth, was totally foreign to the ideas of the trust. It was suggested that a preserved craft could serve as a youth sail training vessel and that the Lord Mayor of Hull, as Admiral of the Humber, might make a ceremonial voyage once a year.

In 1953, the Trust took over an unrigged keel, *Mayday*, from Joseph Rank Ltd. of Hull with the intention of restoring her to her original working condition. To raise sufficient funds for this work to be completed, an appeal was launched and this attracted 200 members. Among those who lent their names to the cause were:- Lt. Col. R. A. Alec-Smith, Dr. R. C. Anderson (President of the Society of Nautical Research), J. B. Bradshaw of Driffield, F. W. Brooks (East Yorkshire Local History Society) F. G. G. Carr (Director, National Maritime Museum of London), T. E. Claxton of Castleford, Capt. G. Curteis, A. Hendry, A. P. Herbert, Lt. Comdr. T. Martin (County Commissioner, Senior Scouts, East Riding), G. W. Odey, M.P., Capt. T. I. Peck, H. Hudson Rodmell, Capt. F. Schofield and J. Arthur Rank.

Life membership of the trust cost fifteen guineas; membership £1 per annum; associate membership 10/- (50p) per annum; junior membership (up to 21 years of age) 2/6 (12½p).

The *Mayday* had been built by Richard Dunston and Co. Ltd. of Thorne in 1900 for the Doncaster firm of Thomas Hanley and Co. Ltd. The keel could carry 100 tons and traded under sail, carrying mostly flour or grain cargoes between Doncaster and Hull until 1941 when she became redundant as a sailing craft. Her mast, sails and leeboards were removed, reducing *Mayday* to a 'dumb' barge. She was brought to Hull in 1951 to end her days in the port as a lighter.

When the trust began restoration on the *Mayday*, it was estimated that a sum of £5,000 would be needed to complete the work. The Trust had active support in

Comrade moored at Beverley Beck with the Inland Sailor's Exhibition on display in the hold, Summer 1975.
Hull Daily Mail

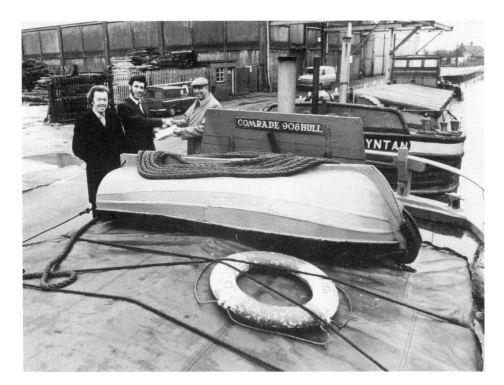

John Hainsworth (centre) Chairman of the Humber Keel and Sloop Preservation Society finalises the purchase of *Comrade* from Captain Fred Schofield (right) in 1974 watched by the author.
Hull Daily Mail

Charlie Gray (left) and George Fussey of the Humber Keel and Sloop Preservation Society with *Comrade*'s new burgee.
Hull Daily Mail

raising this money from the North Eastern branch of the Inland Waterways Association, who had Patrick Wall, M.P. as their patron. It was said that York Corporation had offered a permanent berth on the River Foss in the shadow of York Castle when *Mayday* was not being used.

She was brought from Hull's Old Harbour to Stoneferry and then towed to the Beverley Shipyard of Cook, Welton and Gemmell for repair and survey. Staniland's of Thorne supplied and prepared the mast of Norwegian fir free of charge. £1,200 was spent on restoring the hull and this was completed in 1955. The *Mayday*, captained by George Holt, was towed out of King George Dock, Hull, loaded with eighty tons of wheat for Furley and Co. and bound for Gainsborough.

No funds remained to renovate the keel's sailing gear, and the *Mayday* was kept in limited towing commission by the Trust between October 1955 and January 1957.

Hull, Gainsborough, Selby, Doncaster and Wakefield were regular ports of call for the vessel during this period, with cargoes of cattle cake, grain, coal, wire rods and palm kernels.

With vague promises of help and further funds, the *Mayday* was brought to Goole. However these promises failed to materialise and she was left to rot away in a timber pond off the Dutch River, Goole. It was an inglorious end for such a fine vessel.

The Humber Keel and Sloop Preservation Society, a totally new organisation, was founded in 1970 with the aims of preserving examples of both the keel and the sloop and of sailing them in their home waters. In 1973 a fund was launched for the purchase of one of the surviving iron or steel-hulled keels and for its restoration to sailing condition. Original founder members of the Society were: F. G. G. Carr, C.B., C.B.E., L. Clarke FCMS, F. Firth, Dr. A. J. Fouracre, J. Gardner J.P., Mrs. J. Gardner, J. Hainsworth, M. Jackson, Dr. M. J. T. Lewis, The Lincolnshire Association, C. C. Lodge, Mrs. J. Lodge, M. M. Strachan, J. W. Thompson and Mrs. F. B. Todd.

Following a donation of £250 from the Maritime Trust, the Humber keel *Comrade* was purchased from Fred Schofield in Beverley on 16th December 1974. She had been built at Warren's Shipyard at New Holland as the *Wanda* in 1923 for Turner Carmichael of Hull. John Taylor changed the steel vessel's name to *Ada Carter* before Fred Schofield's father, Arthur, bought her in 1929 in exchange for the wooden keel *Galatea* and six hundred pounds cash, renaming her *Comrade*. While being restored she was berthed in Beverley Beck, courtesy of Beverley Borough Council and restoration work was chiefly carried out by Bill Wilson, Jim Thompson, Jim Gillyon, Colin Screeton, Cedric Lodge, Martyn Chalk, Mike Bartlett and Fred Schofield. A mast was provided by Horncastle Developments of Gilberdyke and shipped from Norway to Gunness Wharf on the River Trent.

Finally restored, *Comrade* sailed again on the Humber on 15th and 16th August 1976. A dream had finally become reality, the first time a keel had been under full sail on the river since 1932.

In 1976, generous aid from Lincolnshire and Humberside Arts and from the Science Museum enabled the Society to purchase the Humber sloop *Amy Howson*, owned by W. H. Barraclough. Built by Joseph Scarr and Sons at Beverley in 1914 as the *Sophia* under keel rig for Mr. Scaife. Rerigged as a sloop in 1916, she was bought by Gouldthorpe, Scott and Wright of Grimsby in 1920 and her name changed to *I Know*, carrying market goods and parcels from Hull to Grimsby. In 1922 Barclays Bank sold her to William Barraclough who re-registered her in Hull under the name *Amy Howson*. Alan Hartley, Roy Smith, Rodney Clapson, Les Reid, Cyril Harrison, Dave Robinson and Eric Burton were among those who carried out restoration work at South Ferriby.

On Sunday 14th June 1981, *Amy Howson* sailed on the Humber under full sail for the first time since 1939; a red letter day indeed.

Both vessels are Sheffield size, 61ft 6in in length with a beam of 15ft 6in. Converted to carry passengers, *Comrade* and *Amy Howson* have attended Water Festivals at Leeds, York, Nottingham, Sheffield, Sowerby Bridge, Wakefield, Grimsby, Goole, Bridlington, Beverley, Hull Marina and Thorne, and have featured in films, television documentaries and radio broadcasts; photographs of both ships have appeared regularly in local, regional and national newspapers and magazines.

A full sailing programme is organised every spring/summer and both ships are regularly chartered by individuals and societies. The original aims of the Society made twenty-four years ago have certainly been met.

The partially-restored Humber sloop *Amy Howson* at the
Horse Wash in Hull, September 1979.
Hull Daily Mail

Bill Wilson and Jim Thompson (left) at work on *Comrade*'s mast at
Beverley Beck in the spring of 1976.
Humber Keel and Sloop Preservation Society

APPENDIX

Listed below are some of the names of keels and sloops I
came across during my extensive research:

KEELS

Abbeydale, Abraham and Ann, Acorn, Ada, Agenoria, Ailsa, Aimwell, Albatross, Albert, Alberta, Albert Edward, Alboro, Alert, Alexandra, Alice, Alice Croft, Alice Margaret, Alice and Maria, Alinda, Alma, Alpha, Amy, Ancholme, Anlaby, Anne, Annie, Annie and Ethel, Annie Forlander, Anvity, Ant, Argo, Arthur, Ashcroft, Atalants, Atlkas, Attercliffe, August, Aureola, Aunty Mary, Avis.

Barbara, Barnsley, Barrosa, Beatitude, Beaver, Belle of the Trent, Be Thankful, Bethel, Betsy, Betty, Bex, Brasso, Bravo, Brayford, Brenda, Bride, Brightside, Brilliant, British Oak, Britannia, Brothers.

Calder, Cameo, Carmania, Carrie, Catherine, Cathleen, Cedar, Change, Charles, Charles William, Ching, Chrissie, Christiana, Christopher, Chrysoidine, City of Sheffield, Civility, Clara, Clarinda, Clowes, Comet, Comity, Commerce, Confidence, Coronet, Cranbeck, Cyprus.

Danum, Dauntless, Daybreak, Daystar, Derwent, Diadem, Dido, Diligence, Diligent, Divine, Don, Doris, Dorothy, Dot, Dove, Dux.

Eagle, Ebenezer, Ebor, Eclipse, Economy, Eden, Edith, Edith Annie, Edward, Effort, Eleanor, Elinor, Eliza, Elizabeth, Ella, Ellen, Elma, Elsie, Emma, Emily, Empress, Endeavor, Energy, Envoy, Equity, Eric, Esther, Ethel, Eva, Eva Hewson, Eva and Ellen, Evangelist, Eveline, Excel, Excelsior, Exchange, Exert, Expert.

Fairy, Faith, Fanny, Fanny and Rebecca, Fant, Favourite, Felicia, Fern, Five Sisters, Flare, Florence, Florrie, Forget me Not, Fortuna, Forward, Four Brothers, Fox, Frances, Free Gift, Friends, Friendship, Fruits of Industry.

Galatea, Garland, Gar, George Al, George Adamson, George and Albert, George and Amelia, George and Ann, George and Eva, George and Lucy, George and Rebecca, Gertie May, Gertrude, Gipsy, Gipsy Lass, Gladis, Gladys, Glance, Gleanor, Glide, Godfrey, Gondolier, Goole, G.P. Burwell, Gratitude, Greeta, Guidance.

Hamilton, Hannah and Harriet, Hanson, Harmony, Harold, Harriet, Havelock, Hawk, Henry, Herbert, Hero, Hewson, Hilda, Hope, Hopewell, Houlden, Hudson, Hugo, Humber Witch, Hyperion.

Ideal, Immanuel, Industrial, Industry, Integrity, Intrepid, Invincible, Involo, Iona, Irene, Ivy.

James and John, Jane, Jane and Maria, Japan, Jessie, Jessie and Albert, Joanna, Jock, Johanna, John, John and Albert, John and Allison, John and Elizabeth, John and Hannah, John and Lavinia, John Leach, John and Maria, John and Mary, Joseph, Joseph and Hannah, Joseph and Mary, Joseph and Rhoda, Jubilee, Julra, Juno, Jupiter.

Kate, Kathleen, Kiero, Kim, Kimberley, Kingston.

Lady Ellen, Lapwing, Laura, Lavinia, Leading Star, Leander, Letitia, Lena, Lenroy, Leo, Liberal, Lille, Lilly, Lily, Lily Dale, Lionel, Lizzie, Lorne, Louisa, Louise, Loxley, Lucknow, Lucy, Lucy Ann, Luggie Arthur, Luther.

Mabel, Maggie, Magnet, Marley Hill, Marvel, Mary, Mary Ann, Mary Ellen, Mary Jane, Mayday, Mayflower, Merchant, Midas, Mineral, Minerva, Minion, Minnie, Minnie Rea, Miriam, Mizpah, Mog, Montebello, Morning Star, Moss Rose, Muriel, My Elizabeth.

Nar, Nellie, Neptune, Newbegin, Newark, New Blessing, Newington, Nightingale, Nil Desperandum, Nile, Noble, North Cape.

Ocean Bride, Olga, Olive Branch, Ornega, Onesimus, Only Daughter, Only Son, Onward, Otter.

Pageant, Palm, Patridge, Pearl, Peggy Birch, Perseverance, Petrel, Pheasant, Phoebe, Pledge, Polofie, Precursor, Pretoria, Primula, Prince, Prince of Wales, Princess Ena, Priscilla, Process, Progress, Prolific, Prosperity, Providence.

Queen.

Rachael, Radiant, Radio, Ramble, Ransom, Ready, Reliance, Reliant, Rescue, Resolute, Result, Richard, Robert, Robert and Mary Ann, Robert Wood, Rob Roy, Roland, Rollo, Romeo, Rosa, Rose, Rose in June, Royal Lancers, Ruth, Rye.

Sam and Elizabeth, Samaritan, Sarah, Sarah Ellen, Sarah and Martha, Sceptre, Scout, Secret, Sequel, Seven Sisters, Shamrock, Sharp, Silent Friends, Silvery Wave, Sobriety. Sophia, Speculat, Star, Star of Hope, Star of Temperance, Success, Sunbeam, Surprise, Swale, Swallow, Swan, Swift, Sympathy.

Teloc, Temperance, Thistle, Thomas, Thomas Scarr, Thrift, Tibby, Tiger, Till, Titus, Tom, Transit, Trent, Trent Hero, Trial, Triumph, Trio, Try Again, Two Brothers, Two Sons.

Unique, United, Unity.

Valerie, Valiant, Vanguard, Venture, Venue, Victoria, Victory, Vigilant, Vine, Viola, Vista, Vixen, Voluta.

Walkington, Walpole, Warrior, Wasp, Water Lilly, Water Queen, Wave, Welfare, Wesley, William, William and Ann, William and Annie, William and Eliza, William Hewson, William and Jane, Willian and Joseph, William and Mary, William S, Willie, Wilsons, Winifred, Wolseley, Wonder, Woodman.

Xerxes, Yeoman, York, Zitella, Zulu, Zurial.

SLOOPS

Most of these were trading on the River Humber between 1920 and 1950.

Active, Ada Mary, Adament, Adelaide, Adlingfleet, Alan, Alert, Alfred, Alice, Allan, Alva S, Amy, Amy Howson, Anglo American, Annie, Annie Barraclough, Annie Elizabeth, Annie H, Annie Maud, Autumn.

Beatrice, Bee, Bertha, Betty, Bonby, Brickfleet, Brilliant Star, Brittania, Broomfleet, Burgate.

Carrie, Clarence T, Clifford, Clothall, Clyti, Comrade, Cranbeck, Cupro.

Defiance, Dei Gratia, Dekar, Dora, Doris.

Earle T, Ebenezer, Edna, Ellen, Elizabeth, Elizabeth and Ann, Elma B, Emily, Enterprise, Ernest, Ethel, Eva, Eva and Lucy, Ever Ready.

Faithful, Fanny, Faxfleet, Fern, Fleetgate, Fred, Friendship.

George and Sarah, German Anne, Glade, Gleanor, Gravel, Greta.

Harry, Henry, Hilda, Holly, Hope, Hopewell, Horncastle, Humber, Humber T, Hydro, Hydromel.

I Know, Iona, Irby, Iris, Ivanhoe, Ivie, Ivy.

Jack, James and Irene, Jennie, Jenny, John, John and Annie, John and William, Julda.

Kate, Kitty.

Liberty, Lillian, Lillian May, Lilly, Louise, Lucy B. Luti.

Madge Jarvill, Marfleet, Mary Hewson, Masterman, Merchant, Merle, Mermaid, Minnie, Miss Madelaine, Miss Patricia, Morning Star, Muriel, Mystery.

Nancy, Nellie and Doris, Nero, New Clee, New Eagle, Nitro, Noble.

Onward, Ousefleet.

Paradise, Peace, Peggy B, Phyllis, Phospho, Prato, Primula, Promise, Providence.

Resolute, Rhoda B, Rising Hope II, Rising Hope III, Romeo, Rosalie Stamp.

Salvager, Sarah, Saxby, Silvia, Skelfleet, Solfa, Sovita, Speedwell, Spider T, Sprite, Star of Hope, Sulpho, Sunbeam, Swallow, Swift, Swinefleet.

Thistle, Thrift, Toft Newton.

Valiant, Vard, Venture, Venus, Verdun, Vi, Violet.

Walcot, Whitton, William and Arthur.

Zenith, Zenitha.

BIBLIOGRAPHY AND SUGGESTED FURTHER READING

Stuart E. Beck *Ships Boats and Craft*. 1939.

F. G. G. Carr *Sailing Barges*. (2nd Edition) 1951.

Clapson *Marine Models*. 1935.

Dalesman Magazine. January 1958. pp. 580-2; April 1958. pp. 49-50; September 1958 pp. 401-2.

R. Davis *The Trade and Shipping of Hull*. 1964.

Baron F. Duckham *The Yorkshire Ouse*. 1967.

--- *The Inland Waterways of East Yorkshire 1700-1900*. 1973.

--- *Navigable Rivers of Yorkshire*. 1964.

Harry Fletcher *A Life on the Humber – Keeling to Shipbuilding*. 1975.

J. Goodchild *Waterways*. 1973.

John Frank *Mariners' Mirror*. November 1955. pp. 308-328.

--- *Mariners' Mirror*. August 1958. pp. 216-239.

Basil Greenhill and Ann Giffard *The Merchant Sailing Ship*. 1970.

Kenneth W. Grimes *Yachting World*. May 1956. p. 235.

--- *Inland Waterways Association Bulletin*. July 1965.

Charles Hadfield *The Canals of Yorkshire and North East England*. 1972. Vol. 1.

George F. Holmes *Humber Yawl Club Yearbook*. 1901.

--- *Humber Yawl Club Yearbook*. 1903.

--- *Yachting Monthly*. 1915-16. pp. 54-4.

W. A. King-Webster *Mariners' Mirror*. XIII. 1956. pp. 251-4.

Marine Models. 1935. pp. 214, 233-5, 260-1.

Roger Mason *Plain Tales from Yorkshire*. 1983.

Hugh McKnight *Canal and Rivercraft in Pictures*. 1969.

Sir Alan Moore *Last Days of Mast and Sail*. 1925.

Colin Munro *Sailing Days*. 1974.

J. Priestley *Historical Account of the Navigable Canals and Rivers throughout Britain*. 1831.

P. C. H. Magazine. Vol. 9, No. 1, 1967, p. 29.

Fred Schofield *Humber Keels and Keelmen*. 1988.

Science Museum, *Sailing Ships*; *Ship Models*; *Sailing Ships and Small Craft*, by B. W. Baths. 1966.

Sea Breezes. Vol. 12, 1951. pp. 22-6.

--- Vol. 14, 1952. p. 141.

--- Vol. 23, 1957. p. 319.

--- Vol. 41, 1967. p. 663.

Slabline. Twice Yearly Magazine of the Humber Keel and Sloop Preservation Society. Summer 1974-

A. Storey. *Trinity House of Kingston-upon-Hull*. 1971. Vol. 2.

J. S. Taylor *Two Humber Keels and Their Captains 100 Years Ago*. 1965.

W. Thorpe *Square Sails on the Humber*, in *Ships Monthly*, March 1965. pp. 46-8.

Michael Ulyatt *Barton-on-Humber in Old Picture Postcards*. 1986.

--- and Edward W. Paget-Tomlinson *Humber Shipping*. 1979.

Yorkshire Life Illustrated. Vol. 7 1953. p. 10.

Lotus   Pumps
          020   8686   2231
            "   8760   0007

Lagoone   £29.99

                £19.99